Tempo

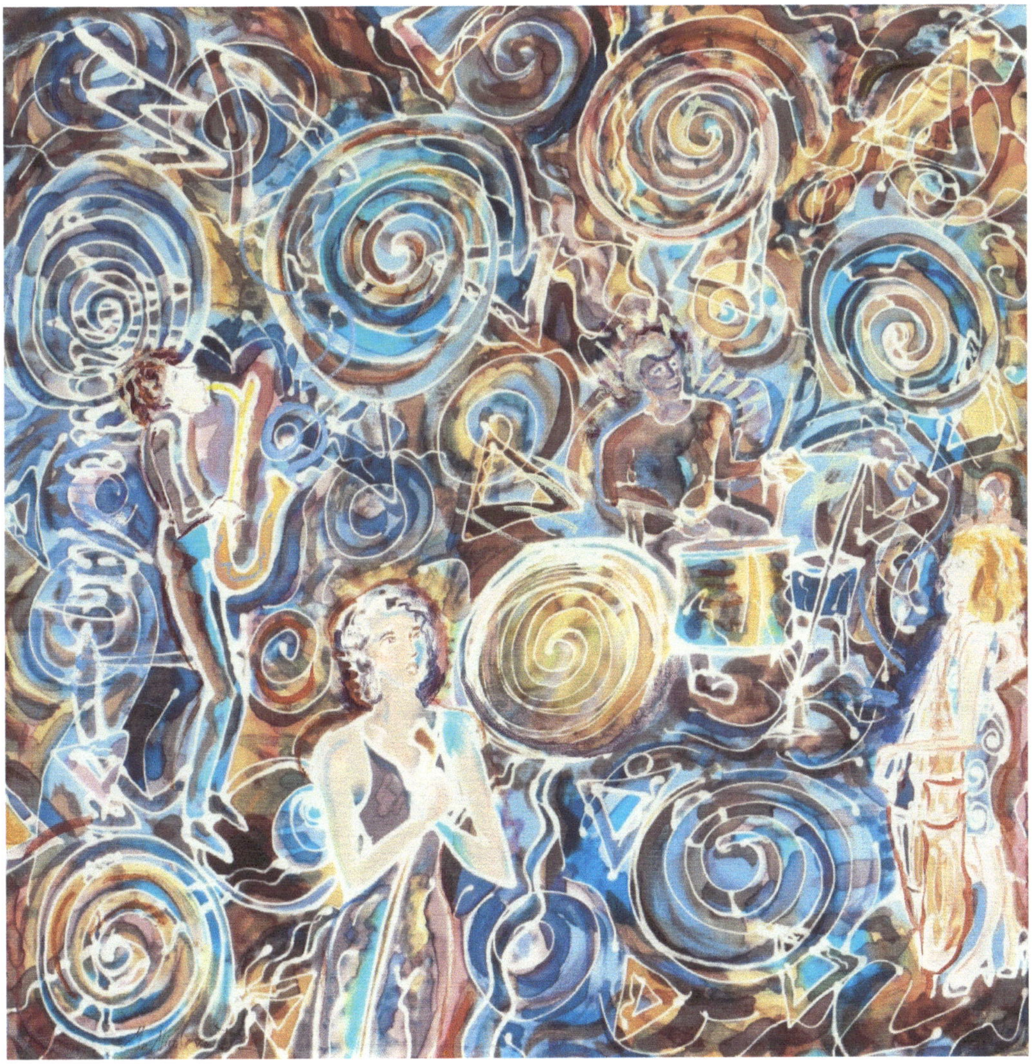

The Rhythm & Rhyme of the Artist

BY M. NICOLE VAN DAM

Art that makes your heart sing with the memory of what could be....

We hope that you enjoy this book of art, poetry and musings by
M. Nicole van Dam.

Thank You for supporting the artwork and creativity of
M. Nicole van Dam. We look forward to hearing your thoughts.

To contact the artist:

M. Nicole van Dam
P.O. Box 583
Ojai, CA 93024

Email: Nicole@Artimagination.com
Website: Artimagination.com
Blog: Wishes.bz

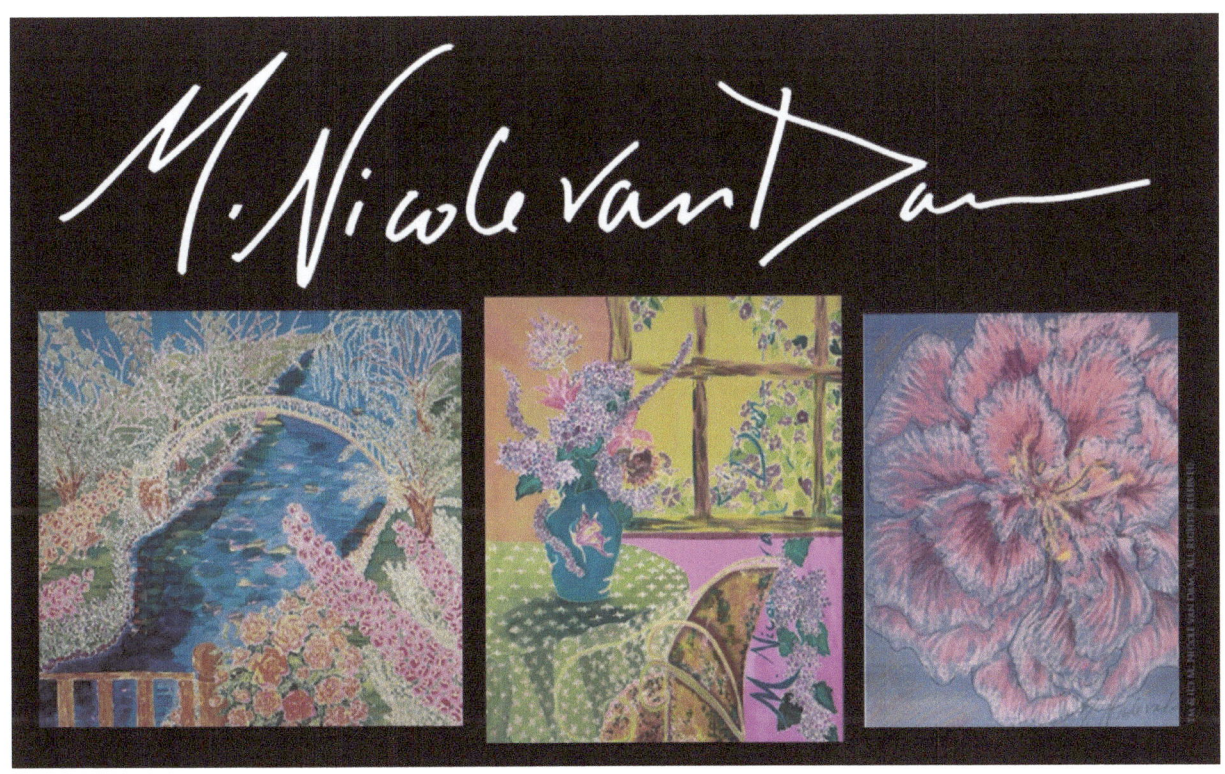

Table of Contents

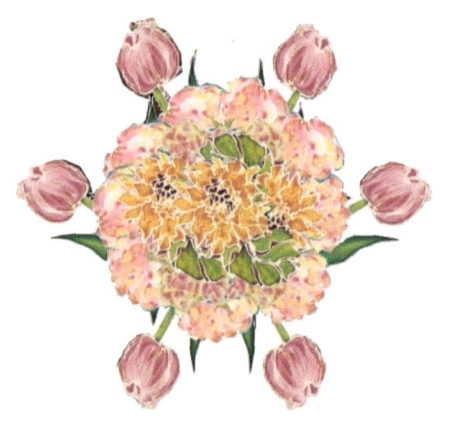

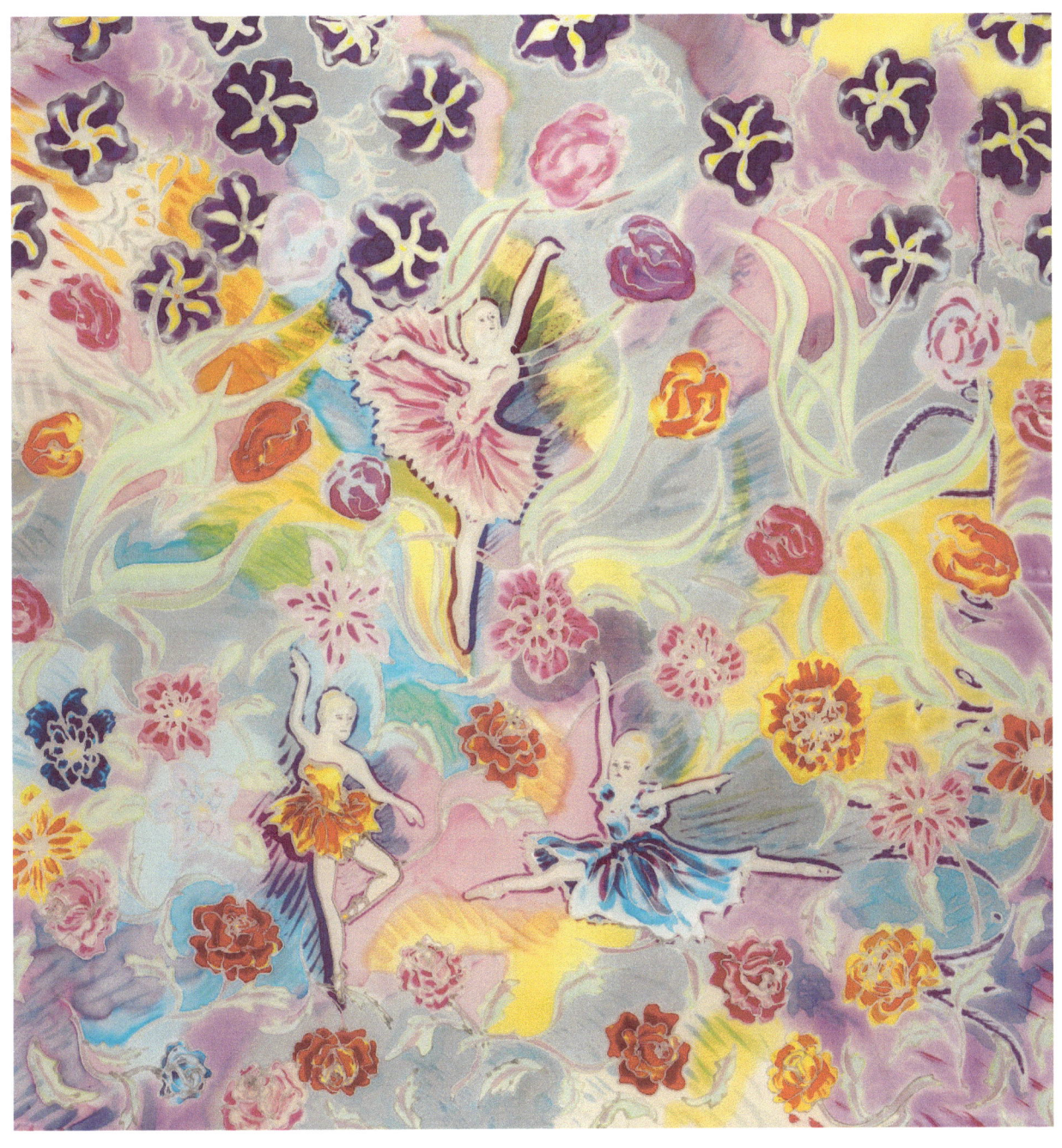

BALLET DES FLEURS
(2007)

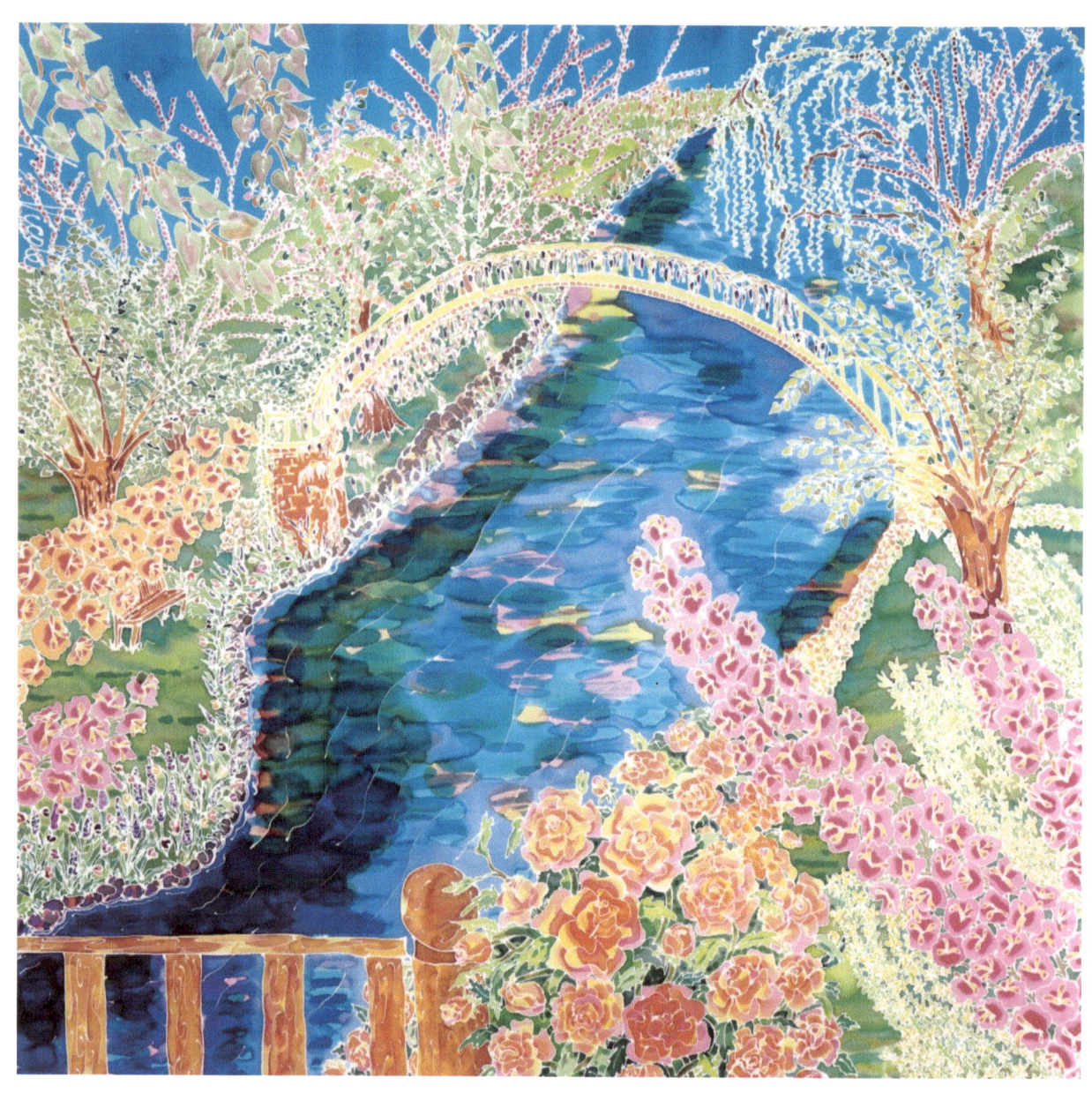

BENCH AT GIVERNY
(1999)

Prelude

My creations are perhaps the best of me, the most optimistic view of me. Through my art I journey from our complex world to a place I better understand, for I have had a larger hand in its making. My canvas, my words, are my sanctuary of solace from weaknesses, insecurities, disappointments, strifes and petty jealousies. My creations are also my way of acceptance and of wishing, of expressing passion, of shouting this is wonderful or unfair, this needs attention, this must be enjoyed or changed.

Through my work I can transport myself, and I hope you, to a more carefree place or to a realm of contemplation. For that is another facet of my work – it is my reaching out to you. I hope my work provides a bridge to my life from yours, from the common threads of that which I have needed to accept, or wish to have in my life, to the complex weave of your past, your present and future. For the brief moments you read my words, you see my art, you are giving my life the gift of blending with yours, and for that, *I Thank You*.

The act of creating is my way of inhaling this life through my perceptions and exhaling through my hands, as intuitive, reflexive and nearly fundamental to me as each breath I take. The decision to create is *not* a decision for me – I would create whether or not people value my creations, just as I would breathe whether or not a given breath I take engenders applause. I wish to create something great in the world's eyes, but even if that is never possible, I believe I shall nonetheless always create for ... it must out. I cannot forever inhale without exhaling, or else some part of me, perhaps even all of me, would surely suffocate.

Creating is automatic and difficult to stifle – I see something and am inspired to celebrate its spirit, borrow from its essence, or comment on its presence. Creating is also my way of sharing my excitement of being with the world, and of being in harmony in our world. In each work, in some way, I comprehend and communicate the soul of what I experience, or what I wish could be. As I create I am lost in that work, in what "is." Oddly, once the work is done, it is almost as if someone else created it – the work becomes akin to a lost photo of a distant vacation unexpectedly found – triggering something real in my heart yet intangible in definition – a slice of a past life captured within four corners of canvas, by its nature destined to shine from that canvas to express the "me" as I was in that moment, to the "you" as you are today. When people like my work it is like a personal affirmation of who I am, at my very core.

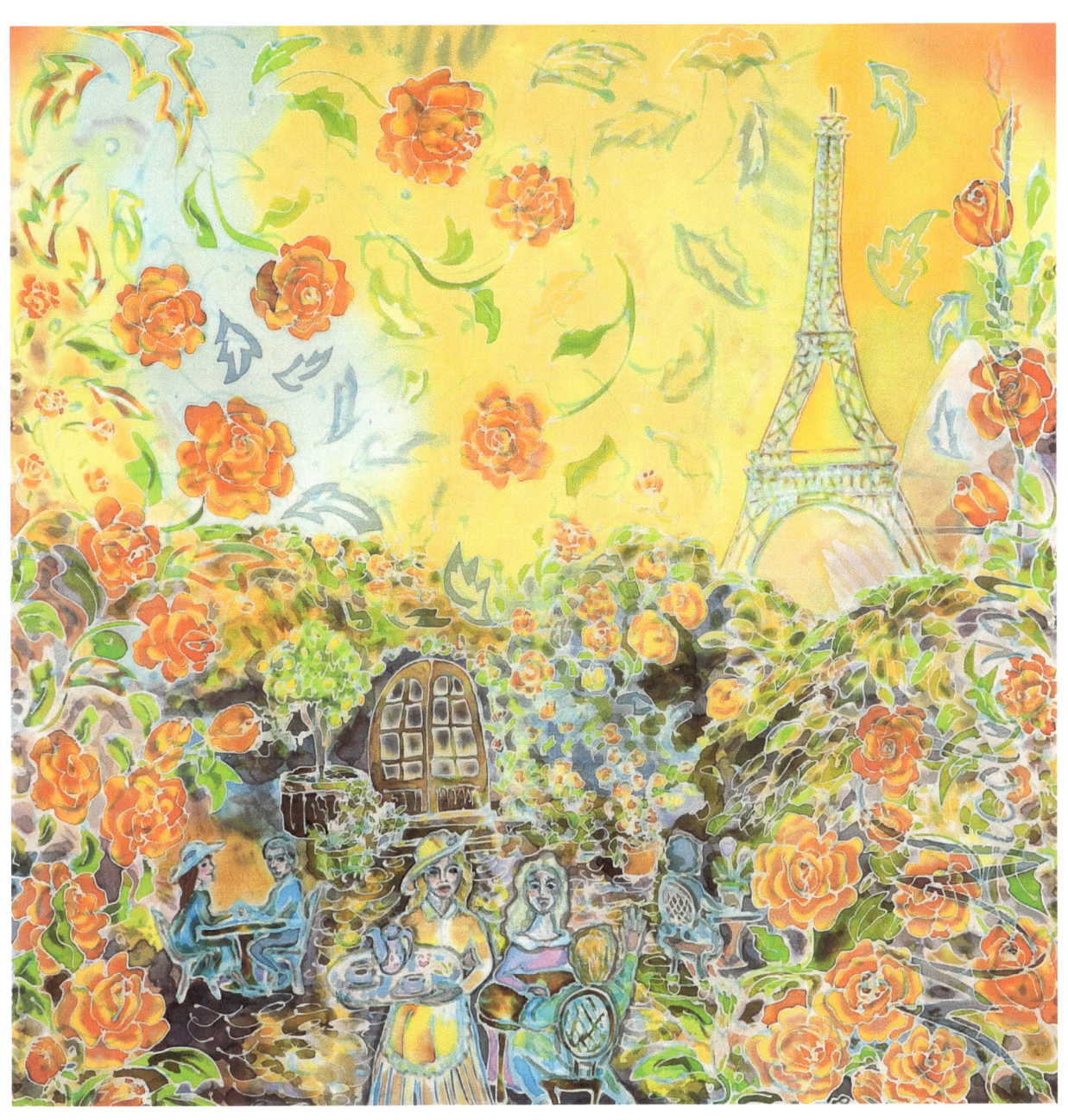

BON JOUR
(2006)

Undiscovered dreams
An unexpected journey
Drifting along memories and hopes
A sweet yearning

Of what could be

  Should be

    May still

All there for my eye to see
In this painting on the wall.

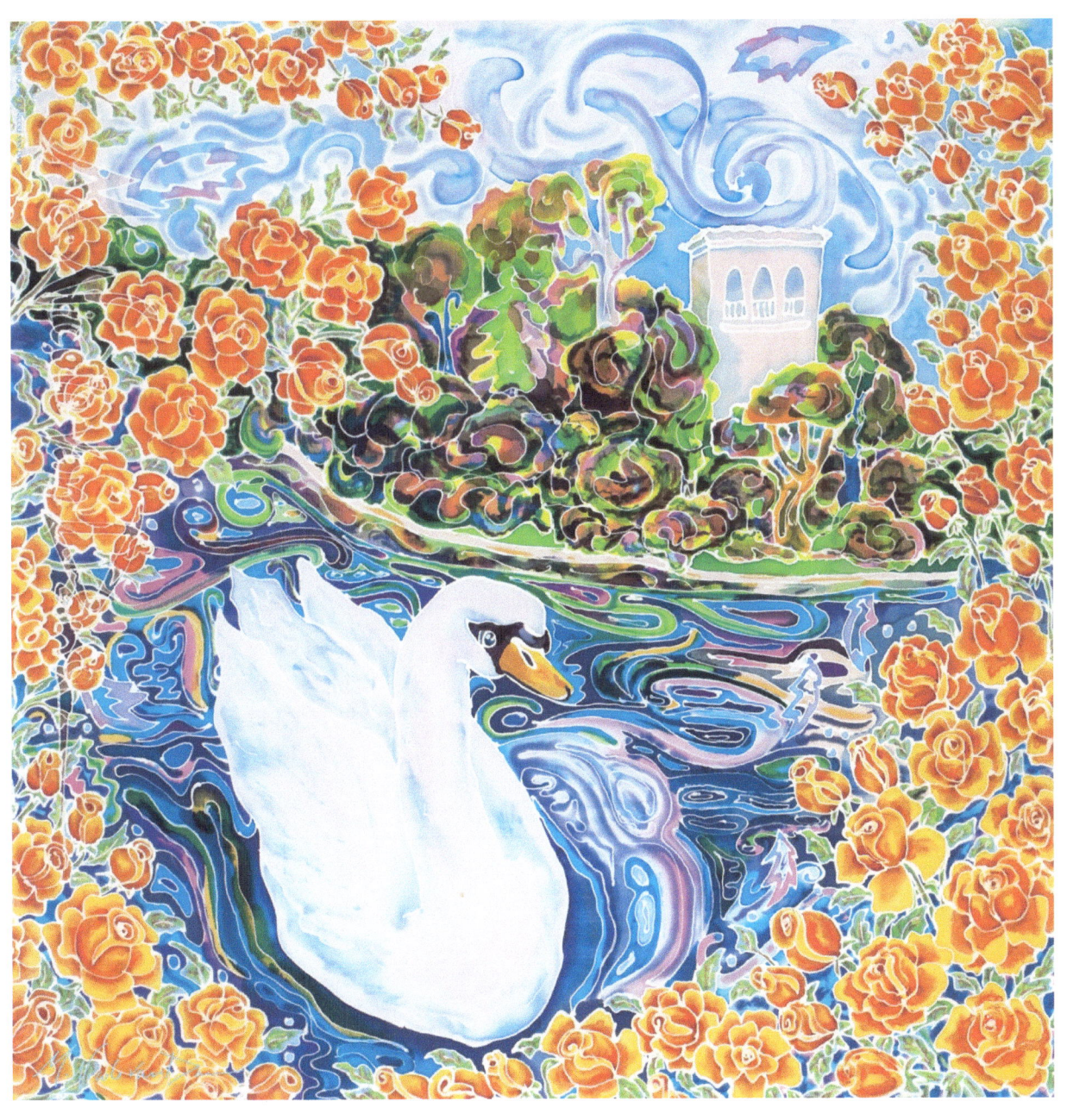

LE LAC DE REVES (LAKE OF DREAMS)
(2010)

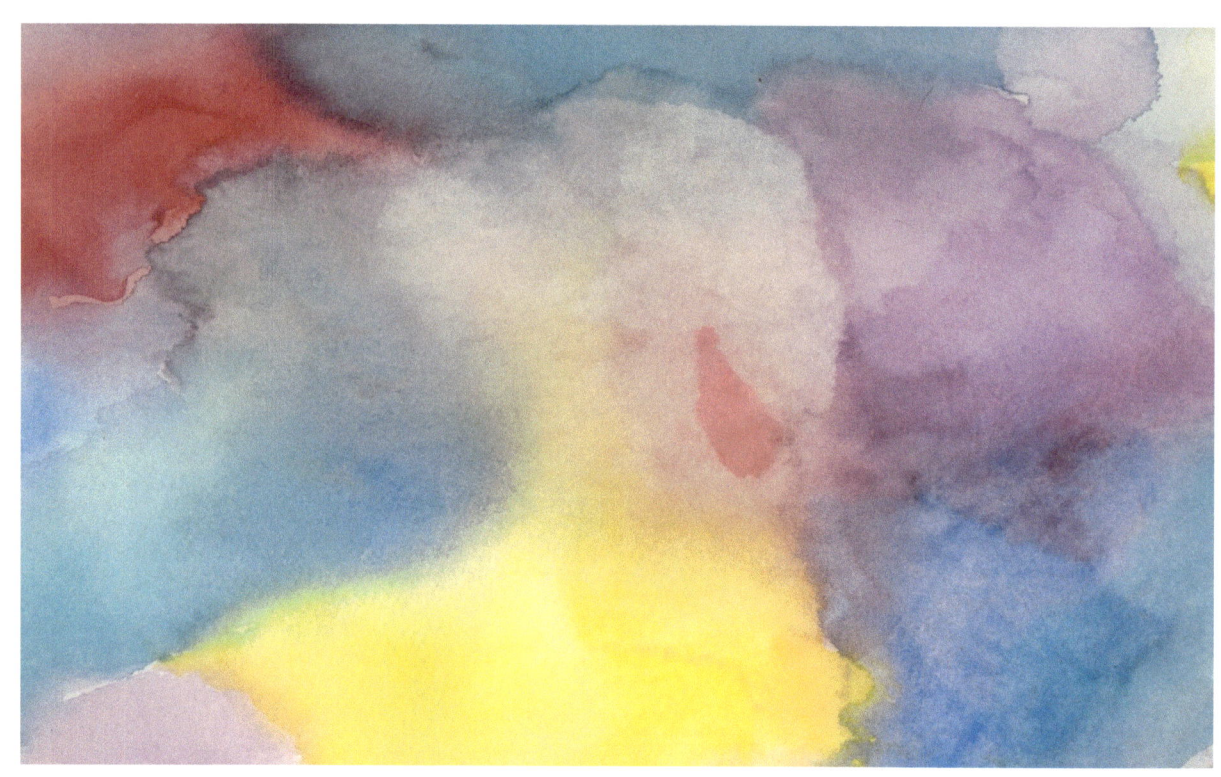

MOODS
(2002)

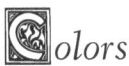Colors

I love colors
I love picking my paints
I love mixing the wonderful blends
I love tints, tinctures and taints
Hues, shades, pales and darks
Glows, glares, fires and sparks

There is such a delight
In mixing a palette just right
In the swish of the brush
In adding just the right touch
Of that daub,
Just the exact amount,
Not too much

Each color has its own passion
Each mixes in just its own fashion
Each has a soul, heart and inner fire
Evoking quiet,
        action,
            foggy distance
                or desire

A pale whitish, rosey grey
Could be a dawn, a dove's breast, or steeple spire
All the same day

If only painted,
Caressed to canvas,
in the apropos way.

Everywhere in life
Palettes unfurl!
I could bathe myself in pastel swirls,
Clothe myself in dramatic twirls
of blacks, reds, silver or gold,
Or house myself in serene blue or whites bold

I love this world, in so many colors dressed
From faded soft denim jeans to white shirts crisp and
    pressed
From cool lavender autumn leaves to fiery summer suns
Chocolaty ice cream to toasty beige buns
The passion of a rose so red
The still misty blue where not a word is said
The cold dark green of an ocean sea
The golden back of a cougar racing free

Colors, wondrous colors
Heaven's gift to you and me
Communication, without a sound,
Of what it means,
  Simply,
    to Be.

We can't always choose what we paint, but we can choose the colors.

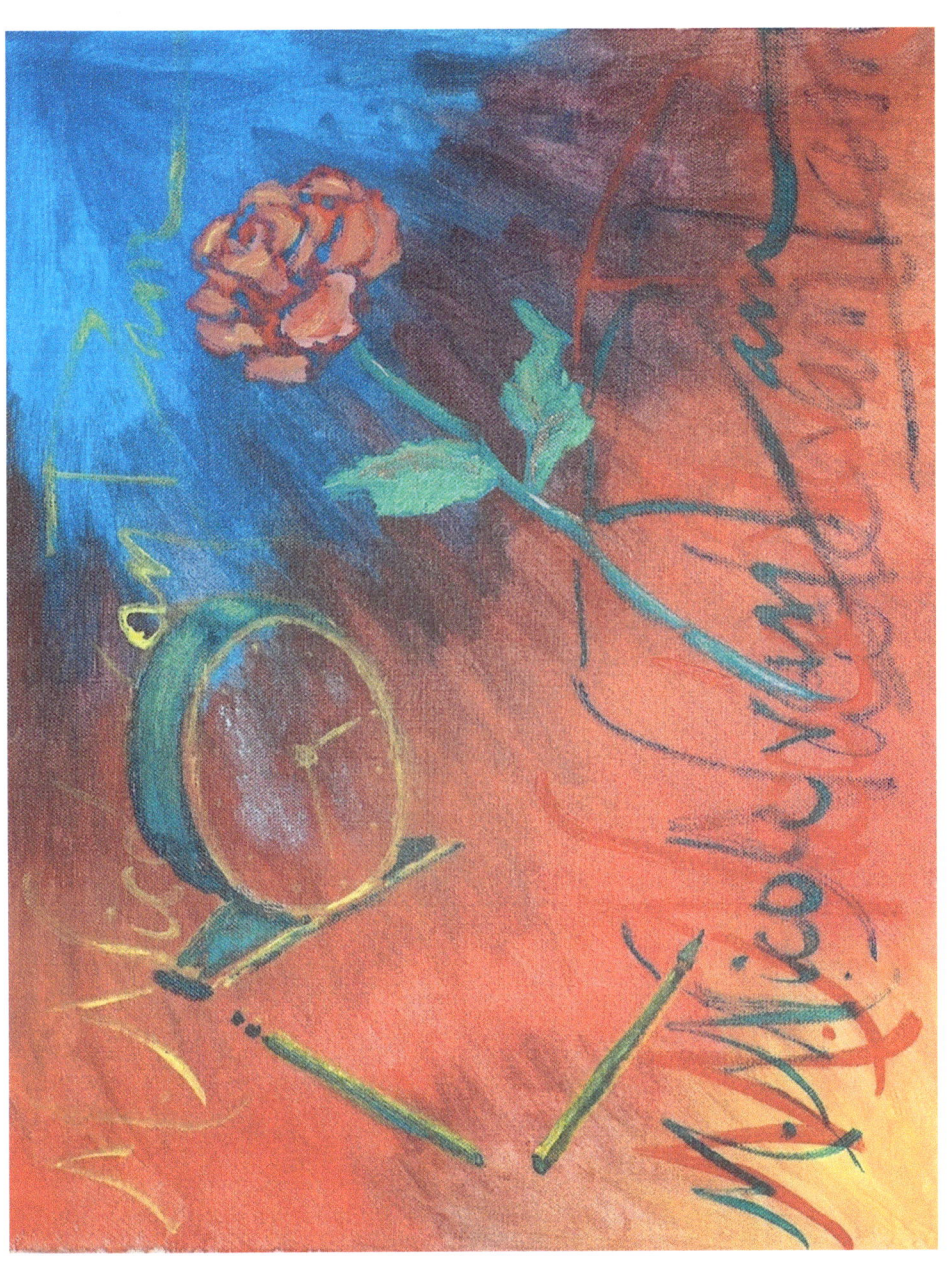

SELF PORTRAIT
(2002)

Allegro

SOCIÉTÉ

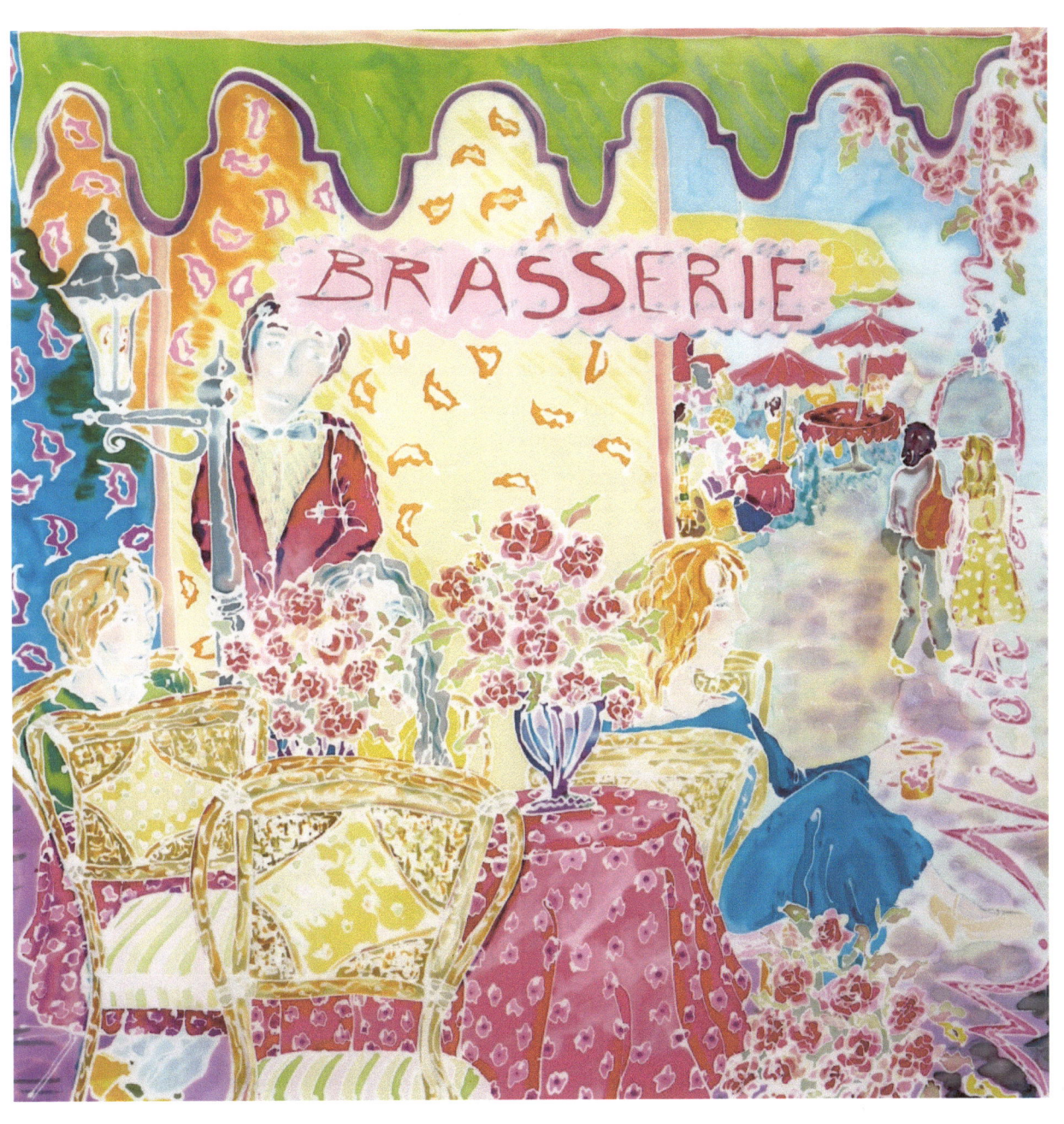

WAITER AT THE CHAMPS ELYSEES
(2000)

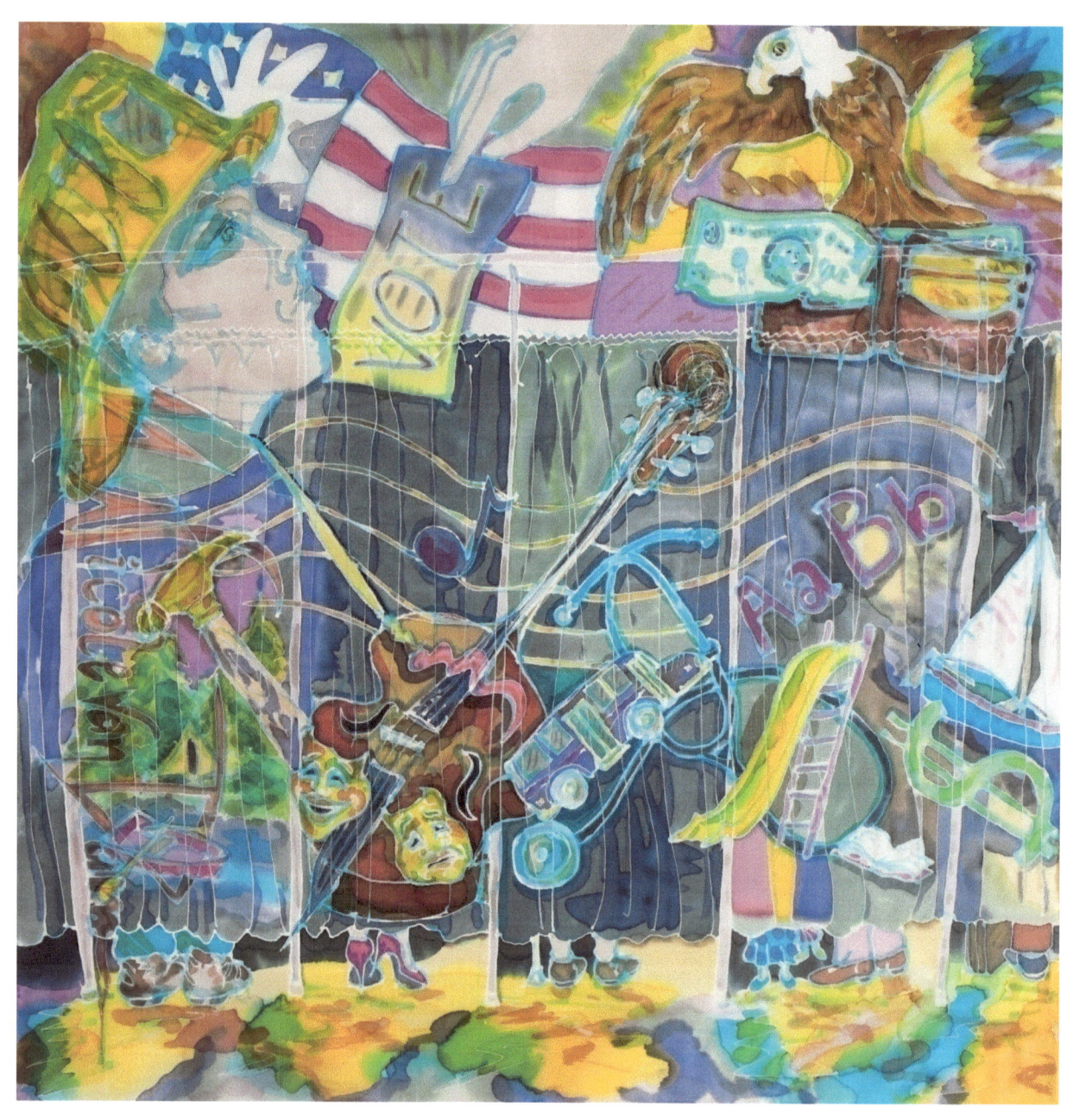

VOTING BOOTH
(2009)

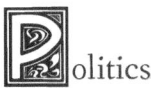olitics

Politics
Humans up to their tricks
So rightfully pretending
Public service never ending
Ethics unbending
All problems mending

These are foes of monetary might
Waging an ad laden fight
With clever slogans to delight
and Red, White and Blue colors always in sight

Each has supporters who avow this candidate is right
The media's twirling spin adds dizzying flight
To a fanciful, murky blend of fact, opinion and insight

The voters hopefully will select their candidate with care
And not in too many false promises be ensnared
Each ballot being cast
Is by an individual among the vast
Populace

But even among the voting throng
Is one common theme to which all seem to belong

A hope that from all this debate comes a vision we can share
Of better tomorrows
An end to the world's sorrows
And a prayer, belied by our experience
That yet

Once elected they shan't forget
All the problems they set
out to fix

In this odd quest
Of debate and jest
Underhandedly above board zest
All at Democracy's behest
Politics

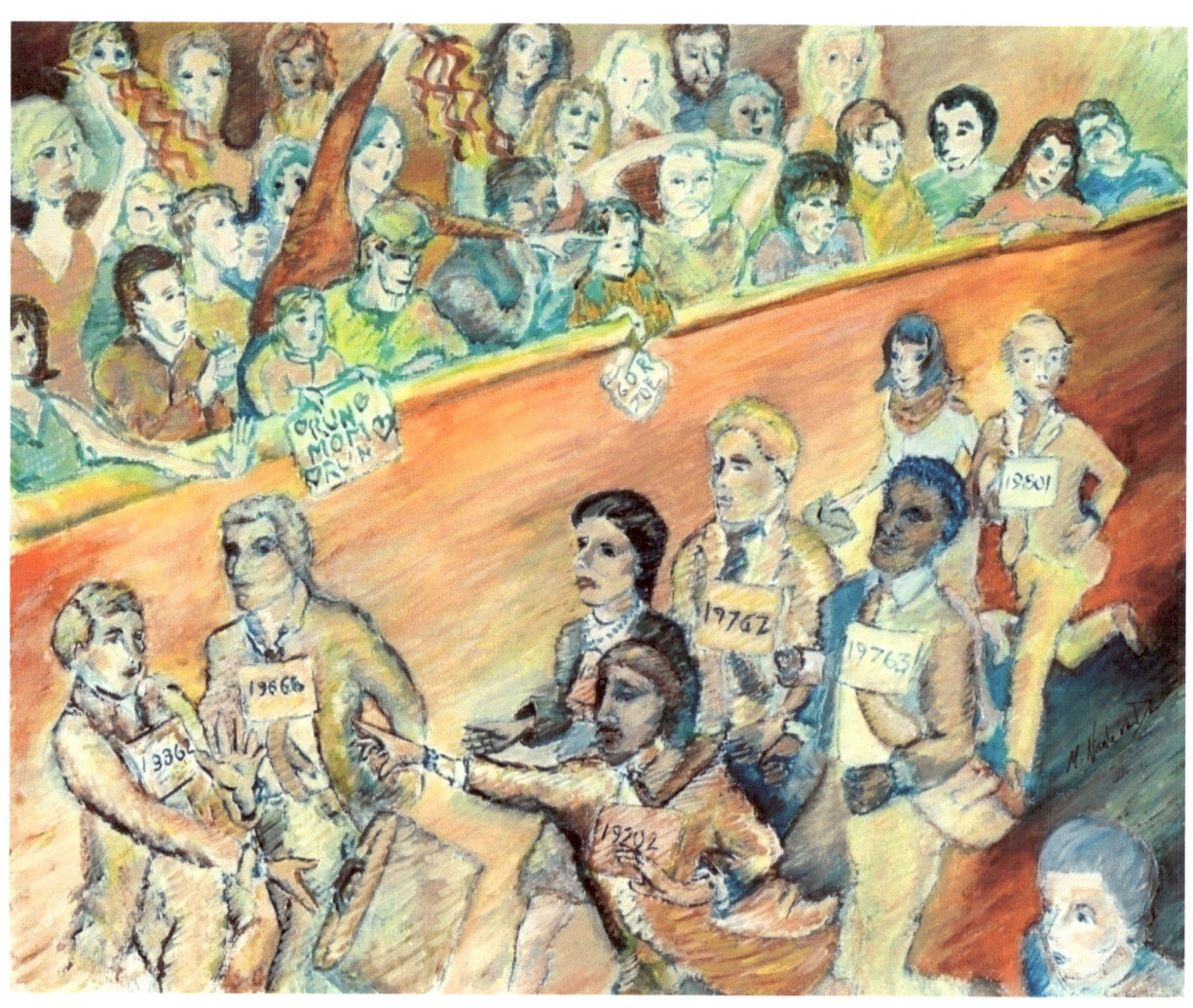

RAT RACE *(2006)*

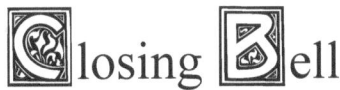losing Bell

The stock market is a mirky place
Intrigue, insiders, ticker tapes quietly floating in infinite
     space
All wait...
The start about to begin...
The bell rings,
The world, red and green, in fevered pitch soars
As each tempestuous trader roars

The market may be up,
   or down,
It almost matters not
Every man for what he's got
A short, a long, a call, a put
Futures at stake
Every day is make or break

Are interest rates up or down?
The price of fuel?
The labor pool?
Can oil go any higher?
Whim or reality, risk or desire?

Is it bear or bull?
Boom or bust?
52 week highs and lows
Maybe the insider knows?
Whispers throughout the din
Everyone out for the win!

Tracking this, weighting that
Be ready when it's time to bat
PE Ratios
Liquidity, cash on hand
Mergers and IPOs
The numbers fly
Be on your toes!

The clock is ticking
The furor rises
Desperate faces wear thin disguises
The closing bell about to ring
Oh no!!!
There it goes!

Shoulders hunched in suddenly baggy clothes
Ill-concealing the day's woes

But not for all,

For some the sun is shining

Cheering themselves for excellent timing

Brilliant work, fast divining

For them no pining

Until perhaps tomorrow

When it begins again

A land of money

Not of friends

Of greed

Not caring

Of me and mine,

Not sharing.

Tomorrow is another day

The only thing is sure

Whether up or down,

Smile or frown

Joy or dismay

It ends the same way.

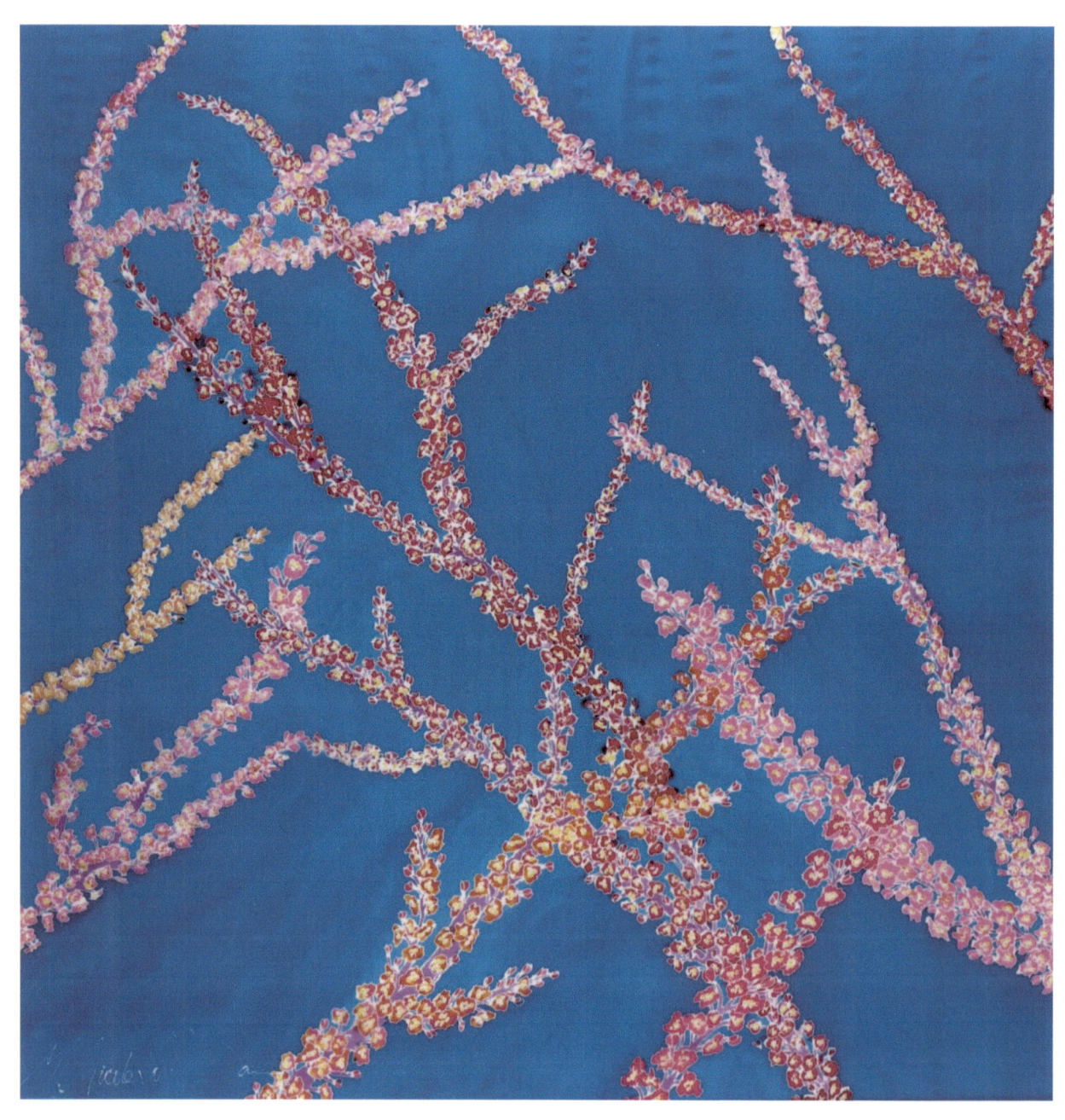

WAR AND PEACE
(2000)

Home Fires Burning

What is Home?
From where did I so far roam?
From cookies in the kitchen, mother, father, child, mate
From weekend antics, a lover's date?
How from there, to this world of hate?

How did I end up in this godforsaken place
Where in bloodshed is Home's gentle grace?
Why did I enlist?
What words could I not resist?

Was I promised a hero's holiday?
Would whispers of a worldwide romp whisk me away?
Could any money pay for this,
Rending me from Home's daily bliss?

Did I swear to defend and protect
That which I now almost forget
In these smoky, death-filled days,
War's inevitable, bloody haze.

Home seems so very vague to me
A worn, worked soldier's foggy memory
Like sands through an hour glass, slipping away
Must the world turn on its head for me to live there again someday?
What Herculean force could bring me from here back to there
Or am I forever trapped in this soldier's fateful snare?

This cannot, must not, be my life
Filled with endless toil, fear and strife
If there is such a thing as Home
Leave me not so alone
Demand my return
Instead of proffering me as fuel for Hell's fires to burn.

I've discovered that one of the best ways to get a vacation from the pain of disappointment or angst is to imagine what it would feel like to not hurt anymore. For that brief instant, I am transported from the painful reality of the moment into a sunnier place.

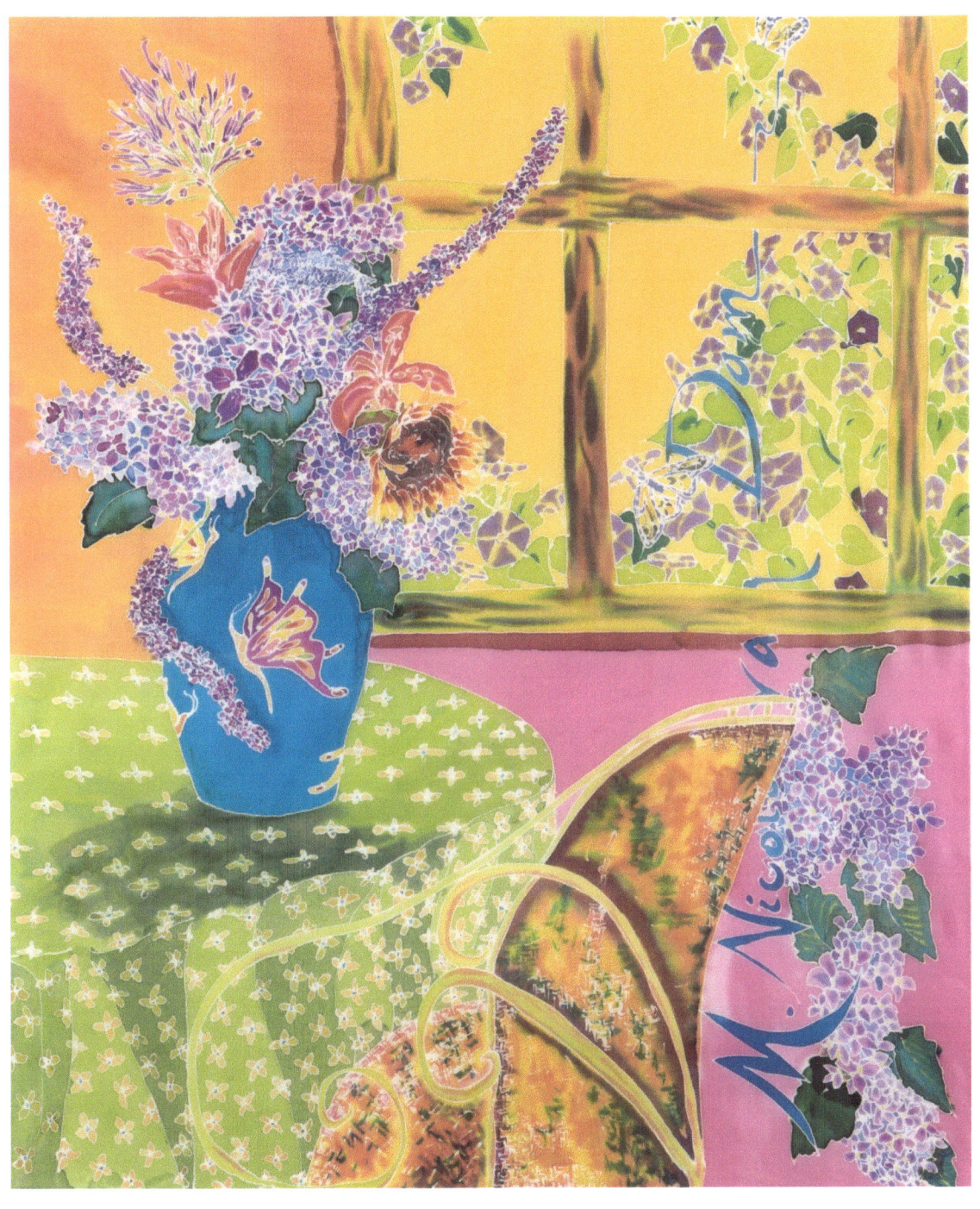

SUMMER AFTERNOON
(1999)

Don this mask and become a stranger,

    an unknown guest

Mirrored in others' eyes the question,

Are You villain, hero, observer, or in conquest?

Here is your visage for adventure and treasure untold
Embark upon this masquerade journey,

Let the Voyage unfold!

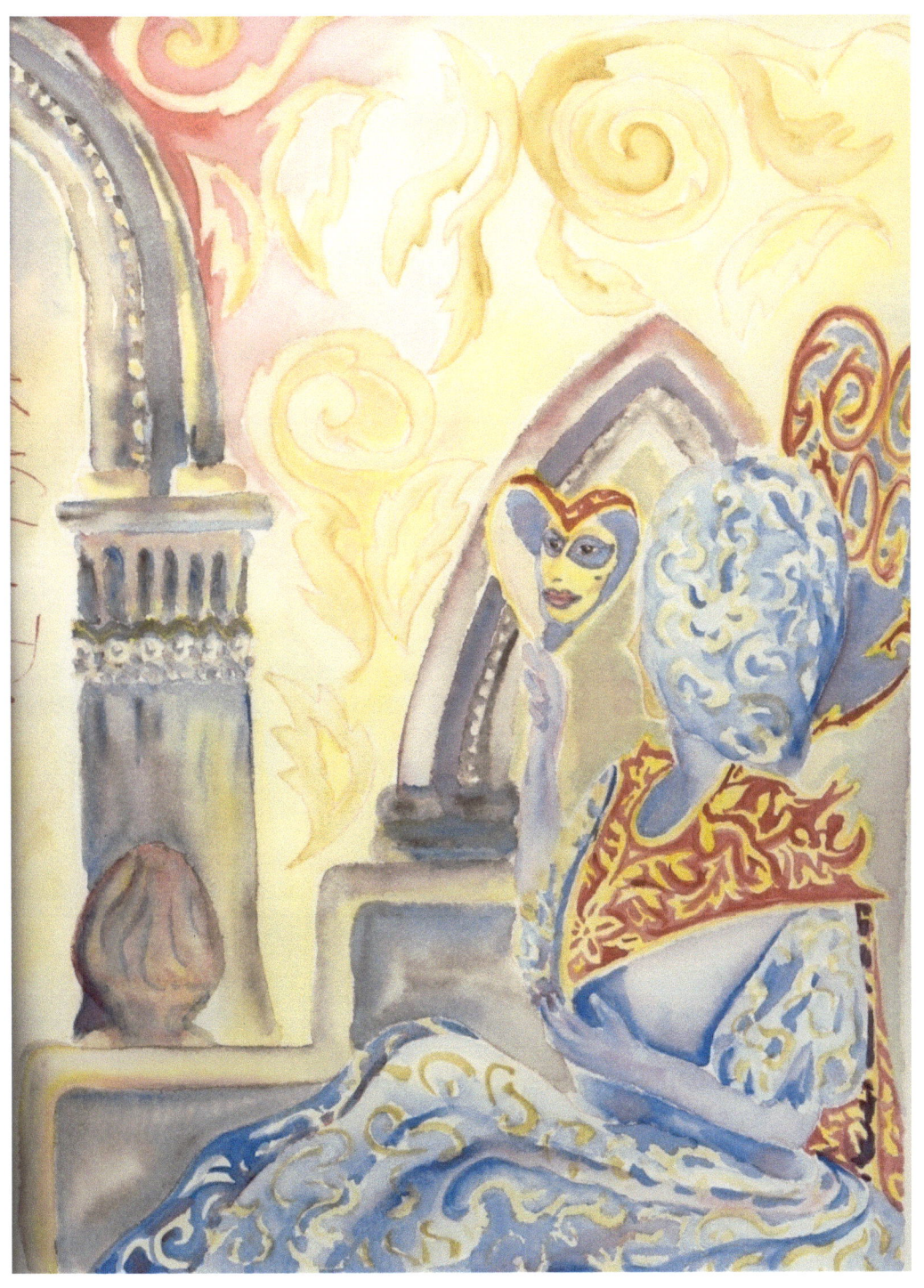

MASQUERADE
Water Colour (2002)

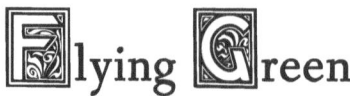lying Green

It is time to be green
Toss the toxic benzene
Past is oil's hour
We don't need crude, sweet or sour
Make way for solar power
Or if not by sun, then by wind or grain
Let's explore renewable terrain

It's time to nurture nature
Call it by any nomenclature
We need to wake up now
Save the earth in Earth somehow

Each of us must do our part
When would be a better time to start?
Recycle, be open-minded, try new things
Let your creativity soar on green wings
There are vast open windows to explore
Once we decide to close petrol's door.

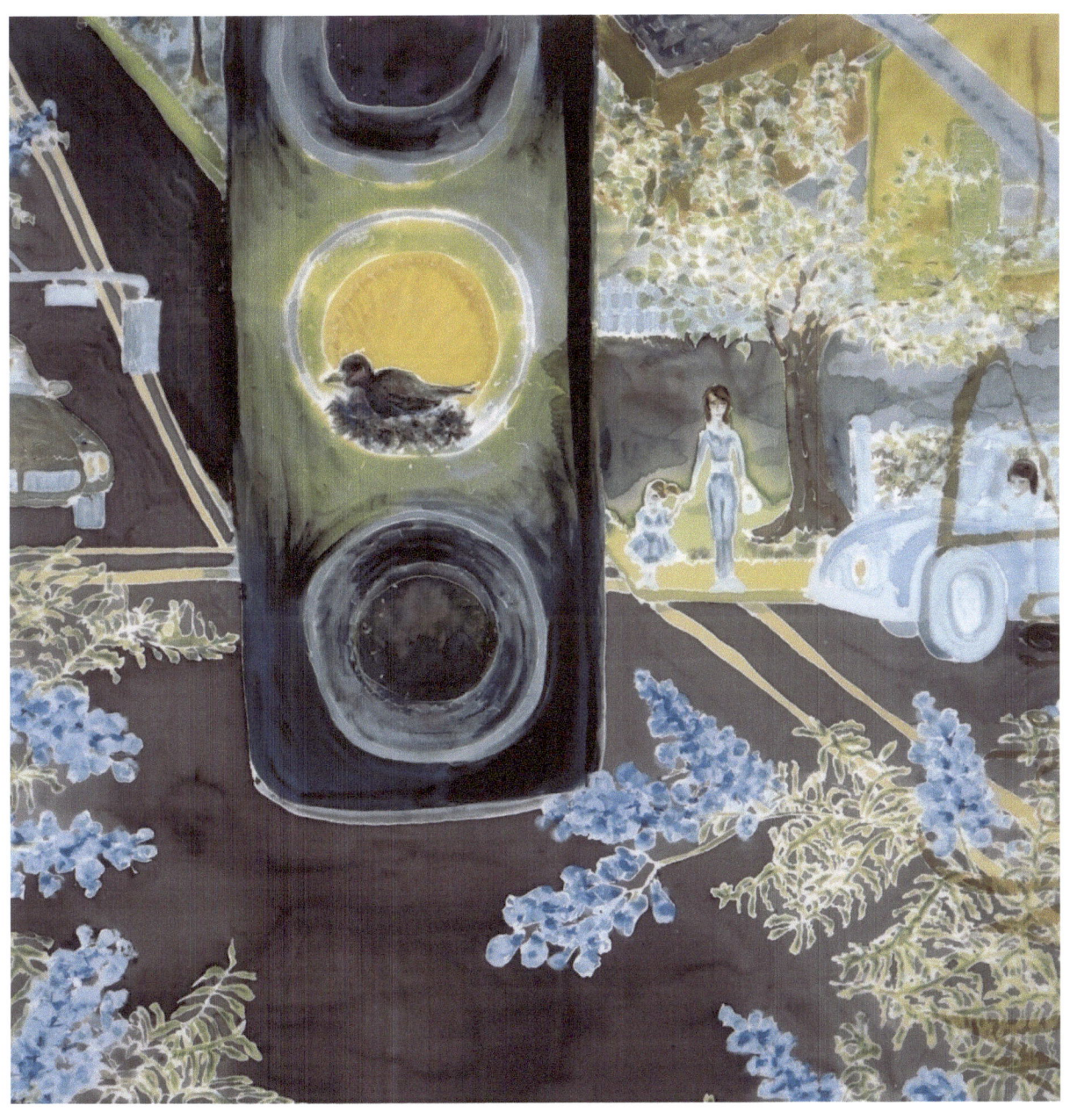

YELLOW LIGHT
(2005)

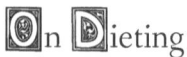On Dieting

Oh the endless craves
How I strive for caloric free days
And when I fail, to not so enjoy the tasty error of my ways
Is anyone truly naturally thin
Able to eat whatever they desire and when?

I hate to diet
I miss my butter
I miss my bread
Must I do this til I am dead?

I want melted decadent choc'late chips
Sumptuously slipping between yearning lips
But somehow never cushioning waist or hips
I want brownies, ice cream and cake
I want guiltless crepes when I wake

I want tea and muffins
Rich sauces and cozy stews
Pizza, pastries and pasta
All without an extra pound to rue

I want the workout without the sweat
The calories burned without the go out and get
I want to be fit and trim
Able to fulfill every edible whim

It's undeniable, it's true
I'm a ravenous hypocrite through and through
So for now, while horrifically healthy food will have to do
I shall relish sinful savory sweet dreams while I chew.

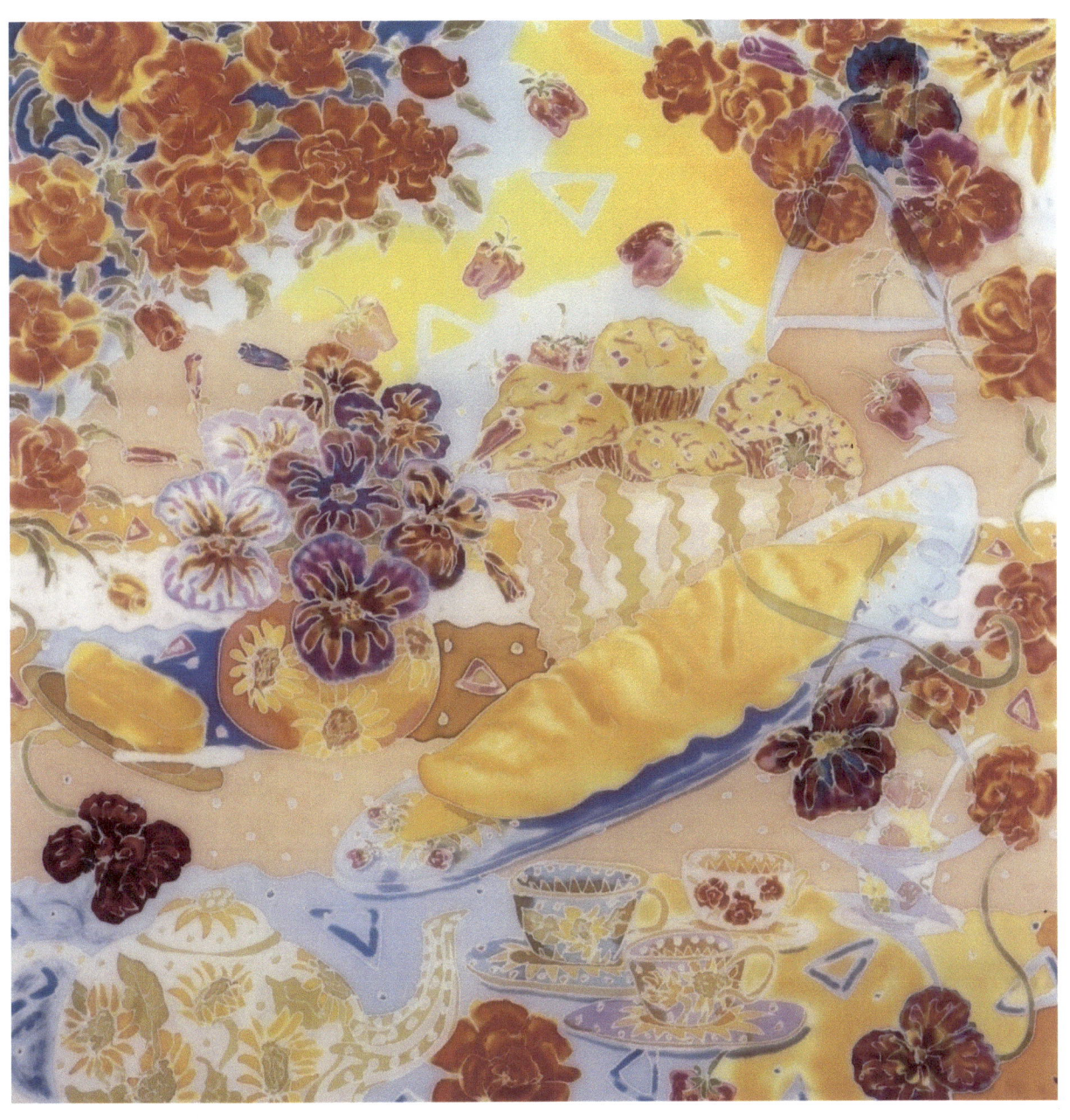

Tea Time
(2005)

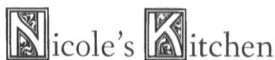Nicole's Kitchen

Aah, the frightening kitchen of Nicole
Where bilious bites find their origins in a bowl
Where her vile concoctions are tossed, ground or disguised as a roll
Her pale gastronomical victims pay their nauseous toll

She calls her fare creative
You might find it permanently sedative
Like a mad scientist with conscience not
Her sinks littered with ingredients accidentally doubled or forgot
Brackish brews bubbling in a questionably cleaned pot
Smelling equally heinous, cold or hot

She'll add yogurt to collard greens
Ice cream to pinto beans
Substitute all things bad for anything good
Nothing ever tastes or looks as it should
As a vegetarian she'll passive-agressively burn your meat
Joke about mixing in a dog treat
Beware, beware her invitation to eat

There truly is no hope for her cooking
Run and hide while she's not looking
Avoid, avoid
That putrid place devoid
Of anything edible
or culinarily credible
The not toothsome
Utterly gruesome
Kitchen of Nicole

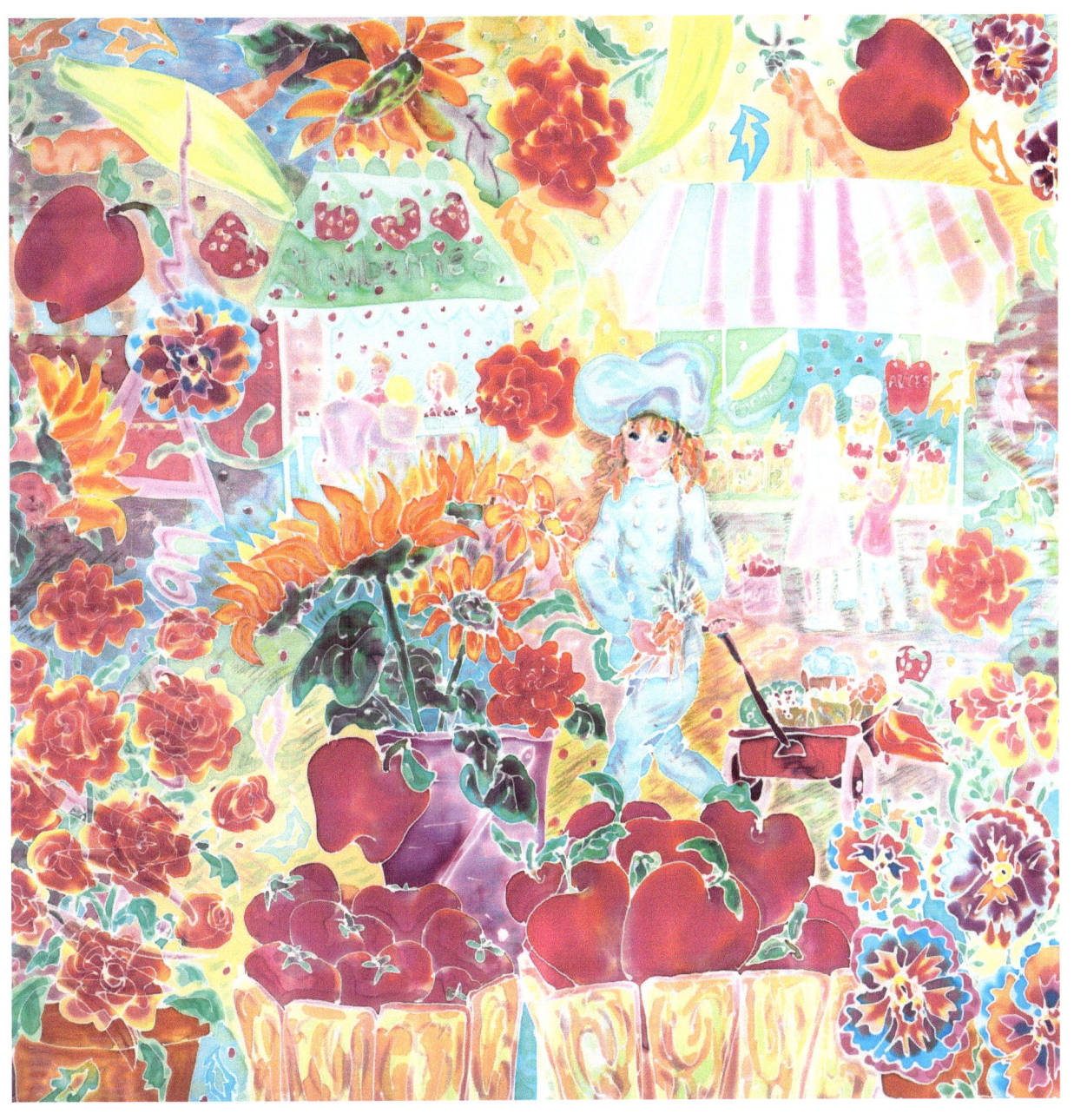

CHEF AT THE FARMER'S MARKET
(2007)

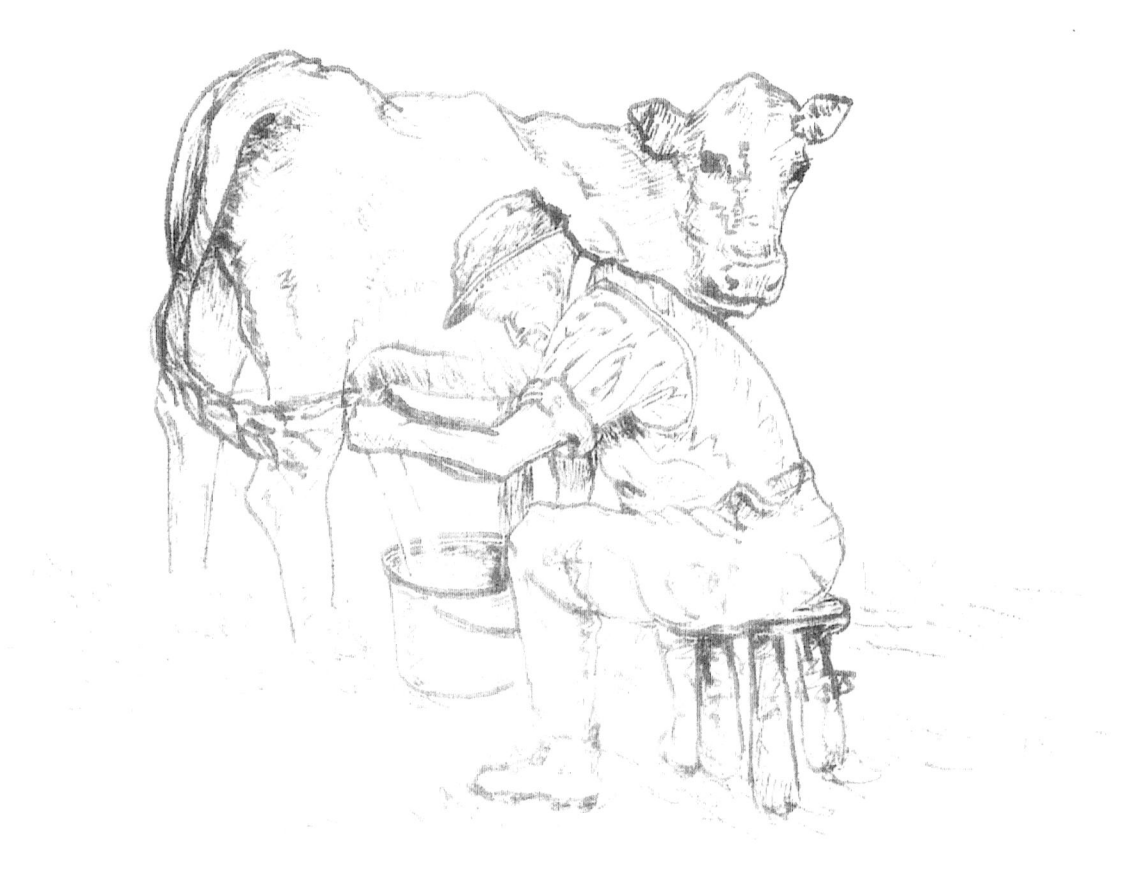

THE MILKER
Pen and Ink (1991)

Anonymous but Not Disregarded

Did you ever measure how many things must die
So that you, only you, must live each day?
I tried to once, and found with dismay
That I didn't think my little life was worth so many others
So while sadly I cannot live and make my life death-causing free,
And while ever so much wish nothing had to die for me,
At least, if I have my druthers,
I can save some of my animal brothers

That piled-high seafood salad I used to eat
Must've cost a hundred lives just to give me a treat
And the veal who began as a baby calf tethered, not allowed to roam
Suffered so that I could have an easily forgotten dinner cozily in my home
And what of the cows whose feet never touch grass,
Stuffed in pens, "living" life in one miserable unloved mass,
Or chickens jailed in tight cages
How many of those did I so thoughtlessly eat through the ages?

I truly believe that if our food in our stores was properly labeled
"Dead Cow who Suffered for You," we would not be so enabled
To ignore their plight
And we just might
Become aware
Of how many things die for us as we laze in our dining chair

Think of how our meat comes tidily hermetically sealed
It looks nothing like anything once alive, whose wounds now cannot be
     healed
Would you really be able to buy meat if you had to see eye to eye
The brown-eyed critter that once was alive?
Could you pull the trigger that led them from farm to table
Wouldn't you be more able
To eat a little extra green
Just so as not to enter that murderous dream
Of that blood and slaughter end to an inhumane life,
Wouldn't you skip a few animal meals to limit that strife?

If you were really truly aware
Wouldn't you care?

I know they say, "But the cows wouldn't be alive except for me to eat"
But once anything is alive, don't we owe it our best to treat
It with respect, just because it shares the earth with us
Isn't that, as the planet's keeper, our sacred trust?

Just because we helped nature an extra cow to breed
Does that mean we have the right to murder it, for food or greed?
And yes, I do believe there are those that must eat meat, but every day?
Must the majority of us live that way?

I wish too, that with the animals it began and ended,
But that's not all in our world we have not yet befriended
Think about how many trees die and how we our forests demean

Just to keep us warm, housed, written, and clean
For the table upon which I eat
For the boxes in which I buy the shoes on my feet
The paper that wraps the presents I give
Must all these trees die, for me to live?

Then there are toxic puddles, clouds and radiated pollution
It's overwhelming, I know not the solution
Except to be aware
To act in a way that shows I care
To minimize the harm I do
And to share what I see with you

I ask myself every day to think
Of how many lives I consume in a thoughtless blink
I know nature and animals still suffer for me every day
I wear leather shoes, drive a car, read and write paper books, aid in the
    world's decay
And heaven help me if veggies have feelings too
I don't know what I'd do
But for now, it is my hope by cutting back if only a little
It is a first step in starting to whittle
The harm I cause, the deaths my needs create,
Hoping with these small changes I spare an anonymous life a dire fate.

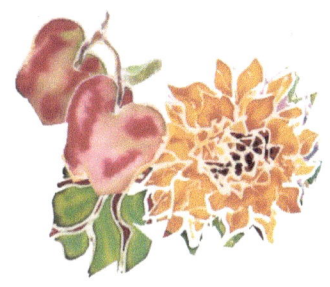

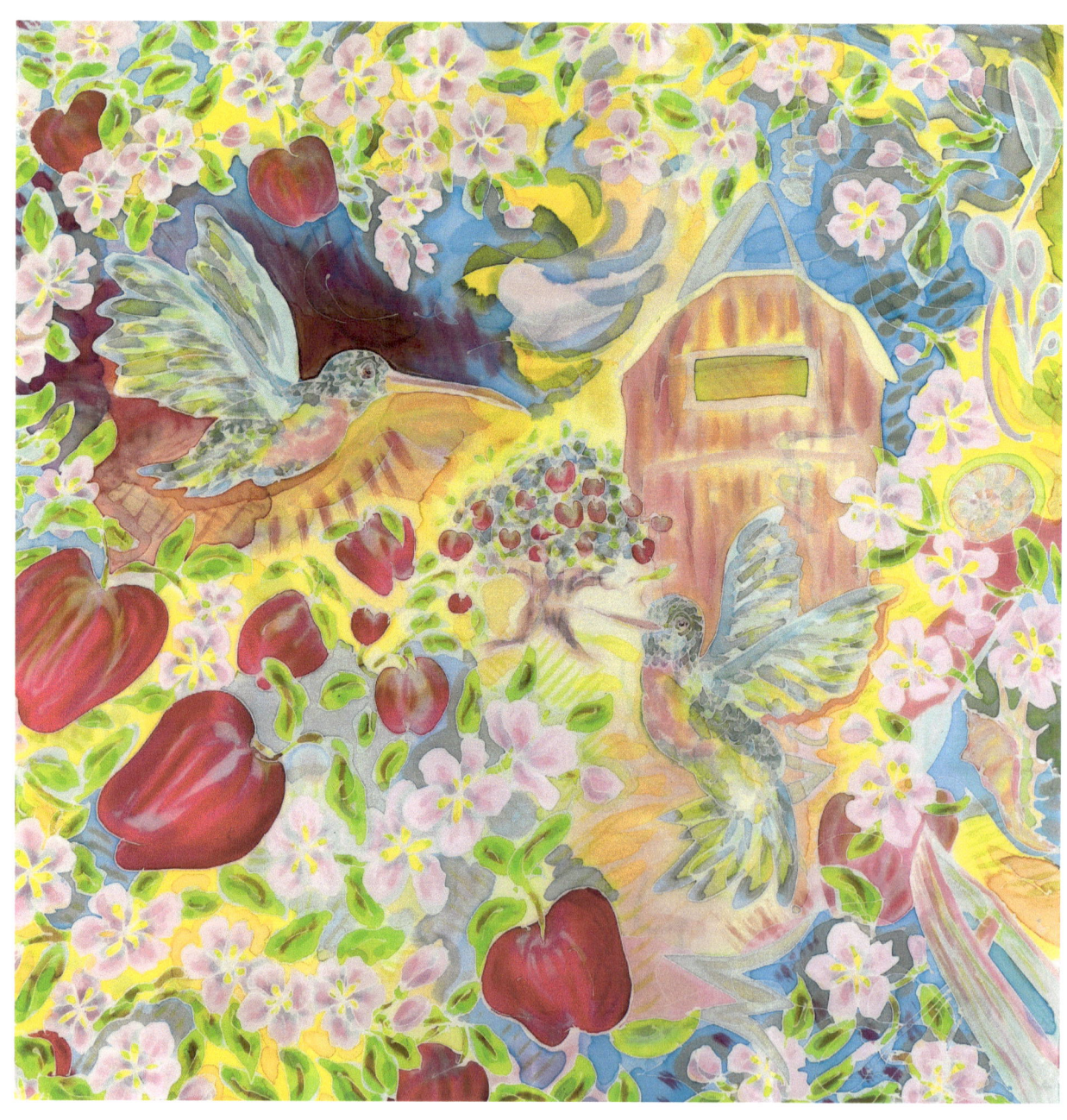

HUMMINGBIRD MEMORIES
(2008)

Ode to the Phone

Do you remember the old dial phones
The kind that really rang
And did not speak in tones?

Do you remember when touchtone phones first came out?
Oh if only we knew then what the devils were really about
Touchtone phones brought to bear
Dial 1 for Automated Customer Care
Dial 2 to find out if you still exist
Dial 3 if your problems still persist
Dial 4 for the menu main
Dial 5 if you are willing to accept blame
Dial 6 if you are returning our call
Dial 7 if nothing else fits at all
To file a complaint, Dial 8
Dial 9 if you want to begin again
If you are confused, dial 10

Yes, my memory goes back further than tales can tell
To the days even before the sacred Phone d'Cell
I know it is a sign of my advancing years, but tis nothing small
I hale from a time when I could actually avoid any phone call

In those days, in the early eons
Phones were not chained to we peons
Free time was really free
My clients, prior cell phones, could not find me
Now they demand, no matter where or when
That I drop everything to speak to them

In the old days
Under the sacred old ways
I could take a trip
Without needing to give lip
service to a boss
I could toss
my cares to the wind
When I was with a friend

The irony is, doctors, once on call
Now are the only ones who rarely give out their cells at all
While the rest of us are burdened with
Cells that make free time a myth.

Of course there are good things too,
About my totable phone d'cell
I can use it anytime, anywhere, to tell
The world to go to h_ll

And more than that
Cell phones come to bat
When the car stalls
For emergency calls
When I am running late
Or alone at a table, cells make a great date
When I just need to say hello
Or when I need an excuse to go
The cell is ringing I say
I must away
Work is calling
The sky is falling

Phones are part of my memories that time cannot erase
And when I die, I'll be buried with one, just in case
Overall, I suppose, could be a worse fate
Than to be paired with my cell as my inseparable mate.

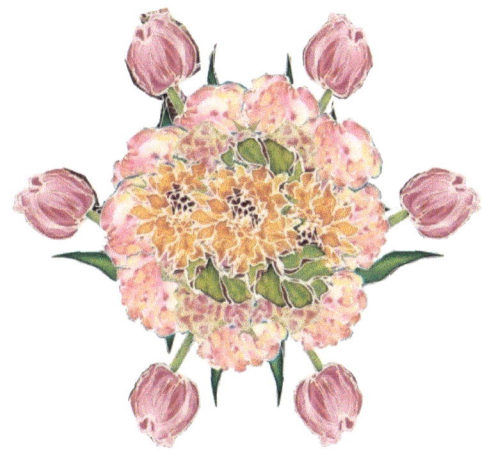

Work is the Curse of the Drinking Class

Now that's a fine thing, this lecture you feed me
All your whining is sure to grieve me
No more on about me working harder
I don't care if I ne'er get any farther
For work is the curse of the Drinking Class
And a Drinking Class man I am

Don't look o'er your glasses with your high society ways
If you could see the world through my bottle you'd be amazed
Life is better through eyes that are glazed
I'll be Drinking Class til the end of my days
For I am a Drinking Class man

Work is the dearth of me drinking time
And me drinking time is fine
I love the pubs, I love me ale
I love it dark, I love it pale
The bottles all long and sleek
It gives rest to the weary, fire to the meek
Aye, work is the curse of the drinking man
And a drinking man I am

None of the fancy drinks for me
Keep your coffee, hang your tea
Give me my beer, or a whisky even better
And I'm your friend, fair or foul weather
Aye, work is the curse of the Drinking Class Man
And a Drinking Class man I am

Don't you start with none of your sass,
I have me friends, I have my lass
So, on a dry day, I'd trade it all for a glass,
And once in awhile I fall on my ass,
Just step aside sister, and let me pass
I'm having another for the Drinking Class!

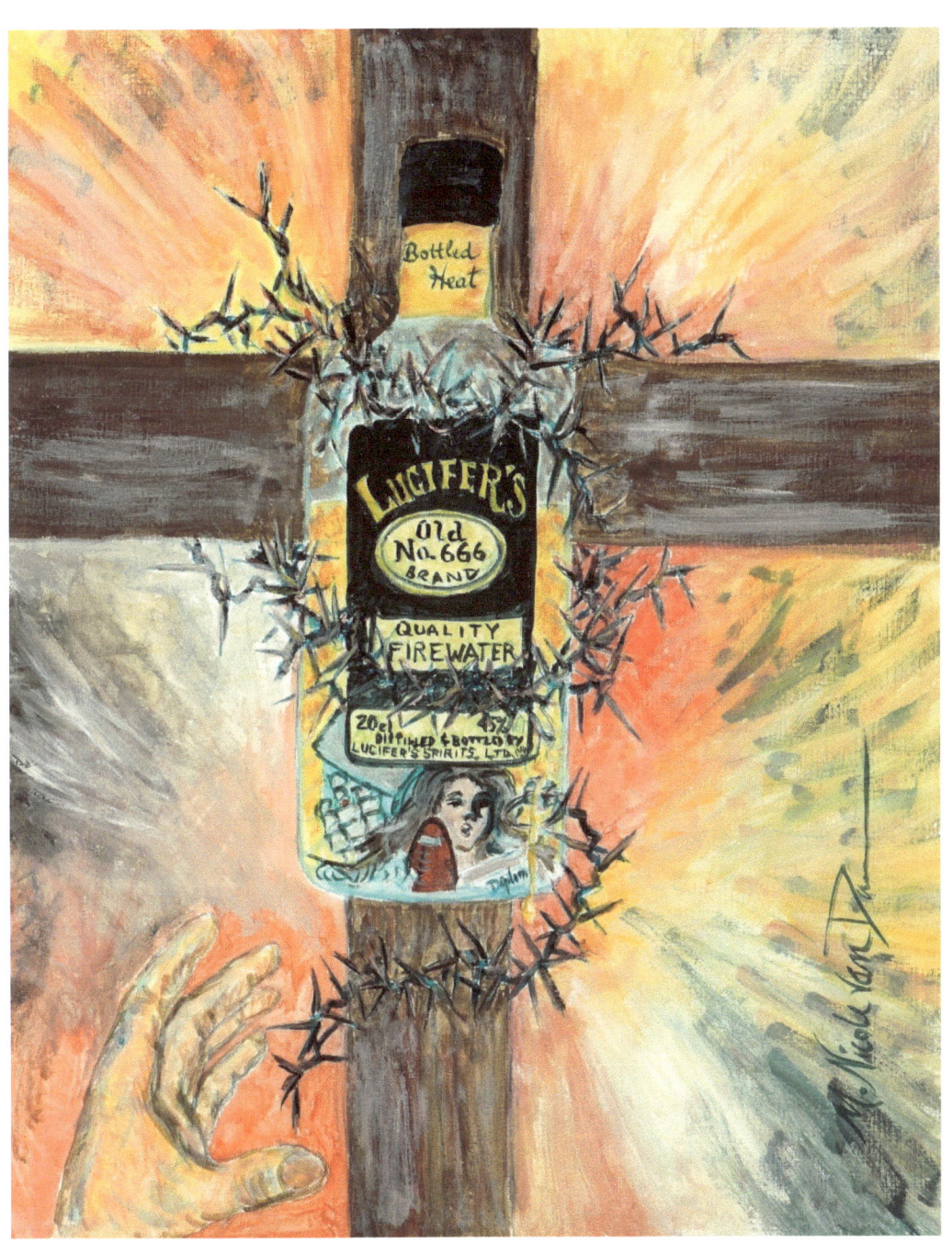

BOTTLE OF DREAMS
Acrylic (2006)

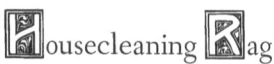ousecleaning Rag

Housecleaning Rag
Housecleaning is not my bag
Housecleaning in fact, is a drag

Housecleaning me
Wishing I were housecleaning free
Aaah such glee
If housecleaning need not be

The vacuum vrooms
Singing brumming tunes
As it suctions up dusty dunes
That clutter up my rooms

Dusting here
Dusting there
Billows of pillows of dust everywhere
Why must there be dust?

Waltzing with my broom
Sweeping muck from room to room
Whistling a merry tune
Brightening housecleaning gloom

Oh housecleaning rag
You could have been a princess' gown
A bride's veil
Silky dress on the town
But instead, like me,
Housecleaning we be
Housecleaning
Housecleaning
Housecleaning
We be.

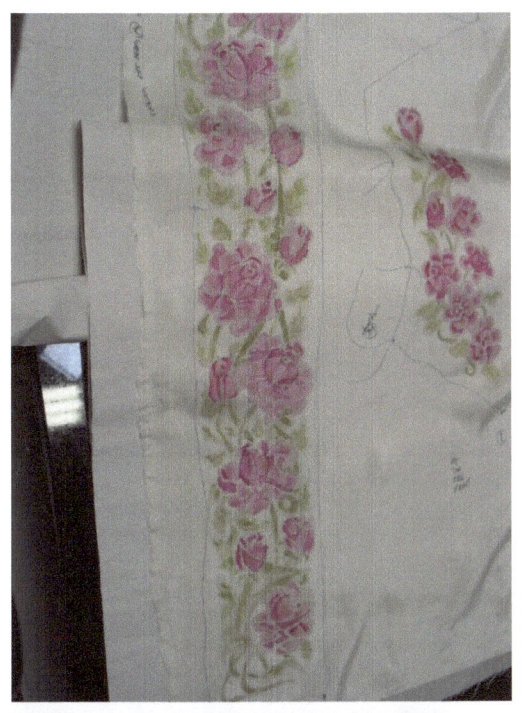

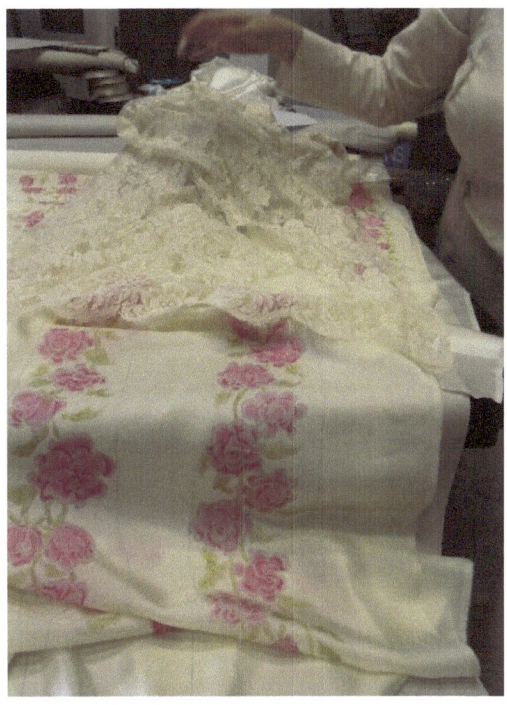

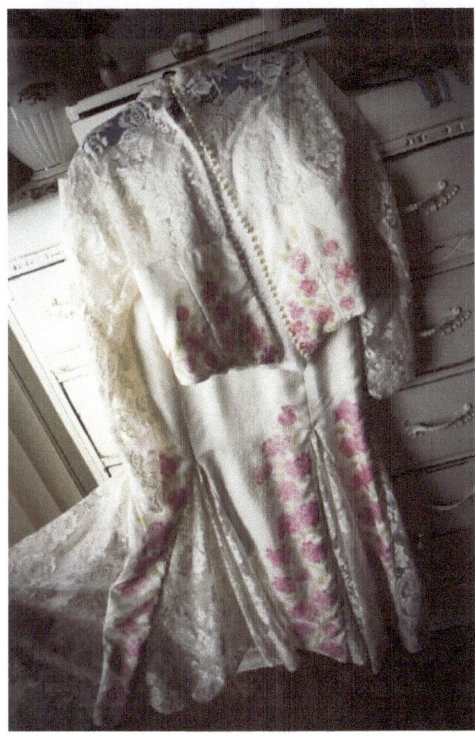

WEDDING DRESS DESIGN & PAINTING

Minuet

Love & Friendship

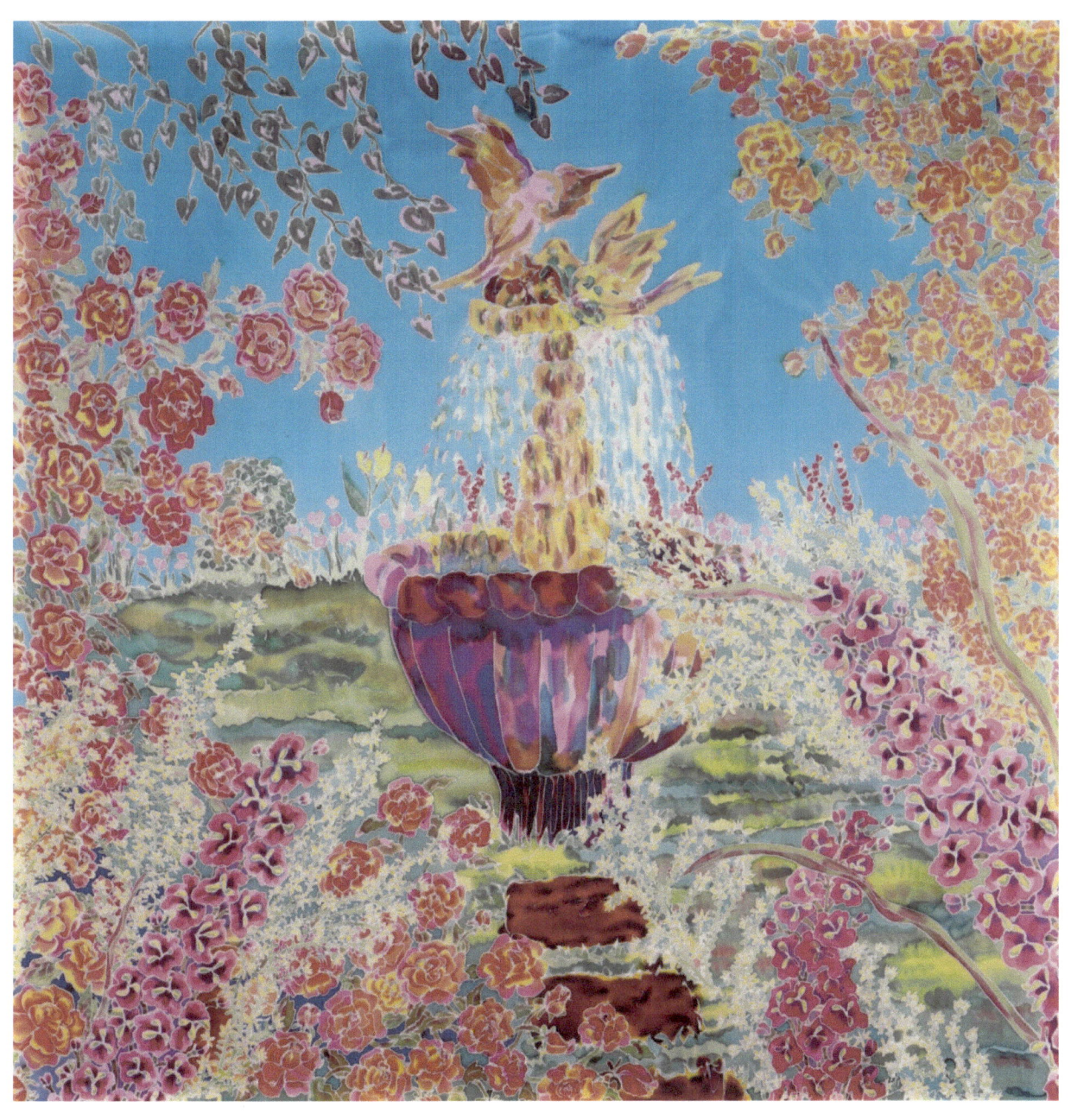

THE WATER FOUNTAIN
(1999)

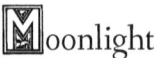oonlight

You're the girl of my dreams
Let's tango on moonbeams
Forever love in sight
Hopes reflections
in the Moonlight

Join me in the stars
Blow a kiss to Mars
Love can be ours
Shine bright..
Moonlight

With one embrace
Begins this dance for two
Heaven's glow
Brings desires in view

I'm yours to excite
You're mine to delight
Moonlight makes it right
Tonight..
Moonlight

You're the girl of my dreams
Let's tango on moonbeams
Forever love in sight
Tonight ...
In Moonlight

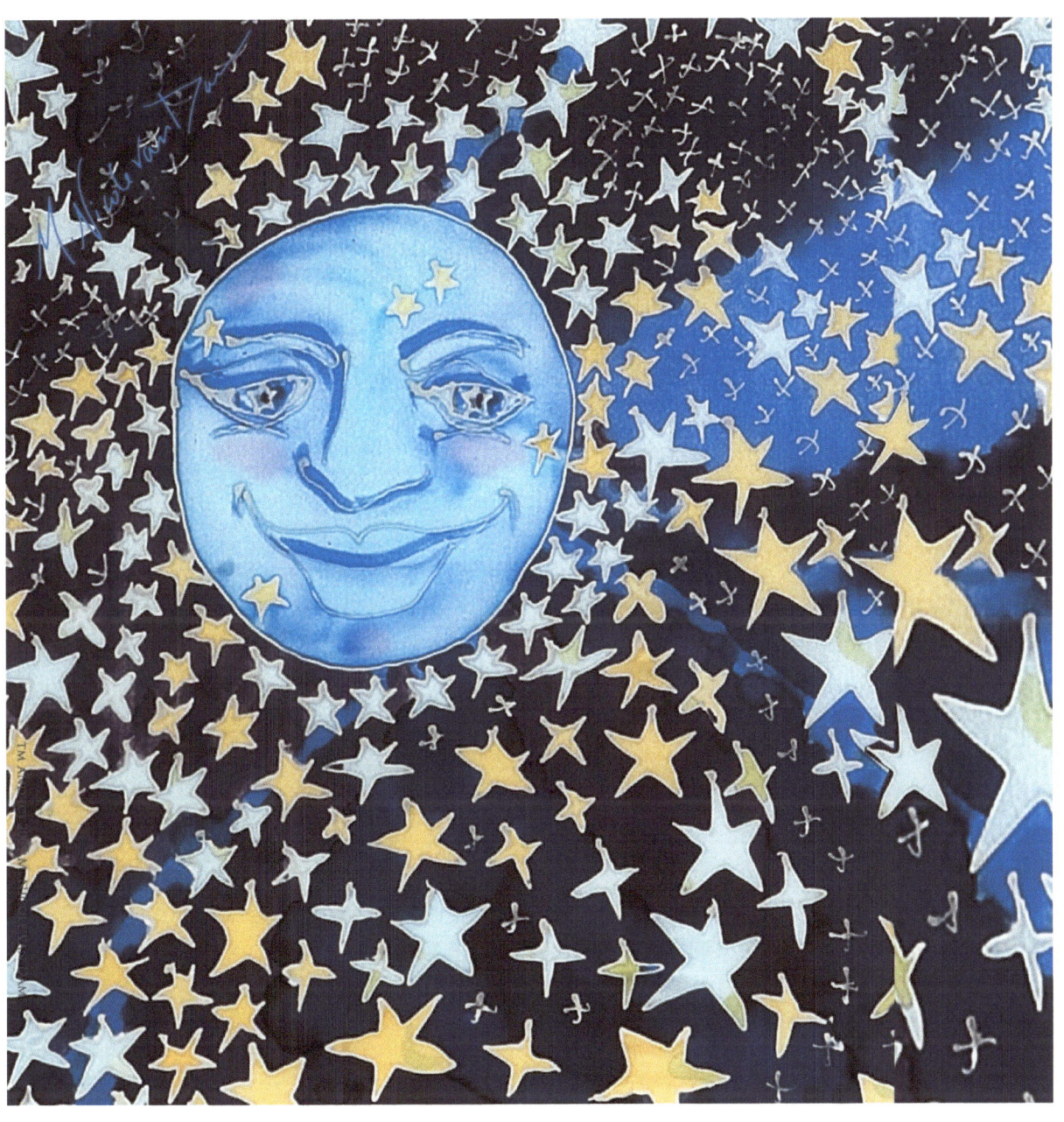

Moon
(2008)

In that secret place

Deep inside your heart

You and your true Soulmate

Are never truly apart.

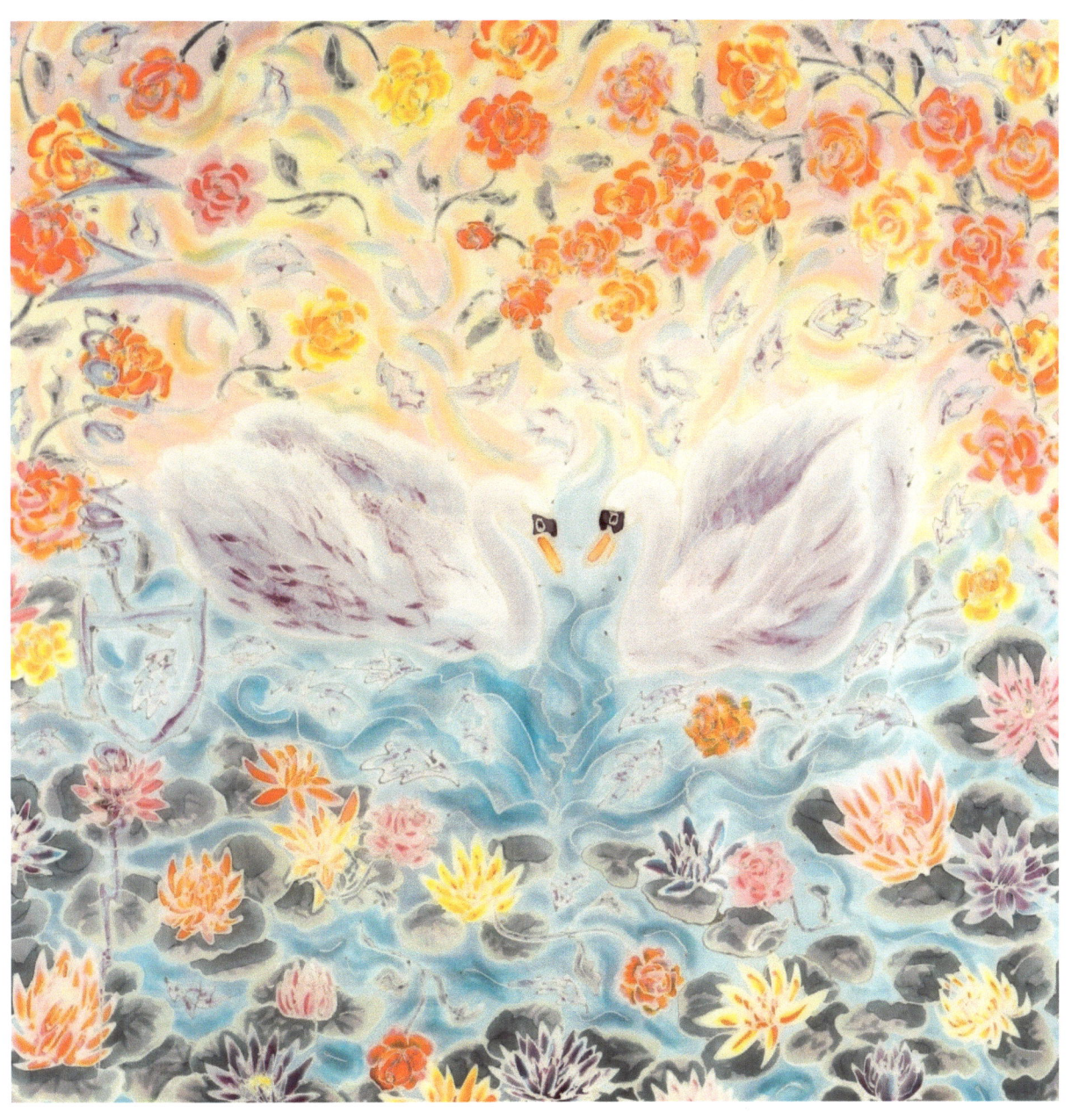

SWAN DUET
(2007)

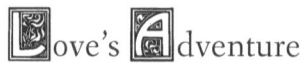 Love's Adventure

Let's zoom through the Milky Way
Zip among the stars
Waltz on tiny Pluto
Tango on Mars

We'll leave Galileo's gravity
For Jupiter's moons
Try Newton's Laws of Motion
Dancing on Saturn's dunes

The Sun on our elbow
La Luna at our toes
Earth above our heads
Soaring with the rainbows

We'll race the comets
To light years away
Stir up another galaxy
Be back in an Einstein day

The constellations will cheer us
We'll pass a shooting star
Throw a kiss to Venus
Soar from near to far

The Zodiac will whisper its secrets
The skies forever we can share
Make love to me my darling
And we will be there.

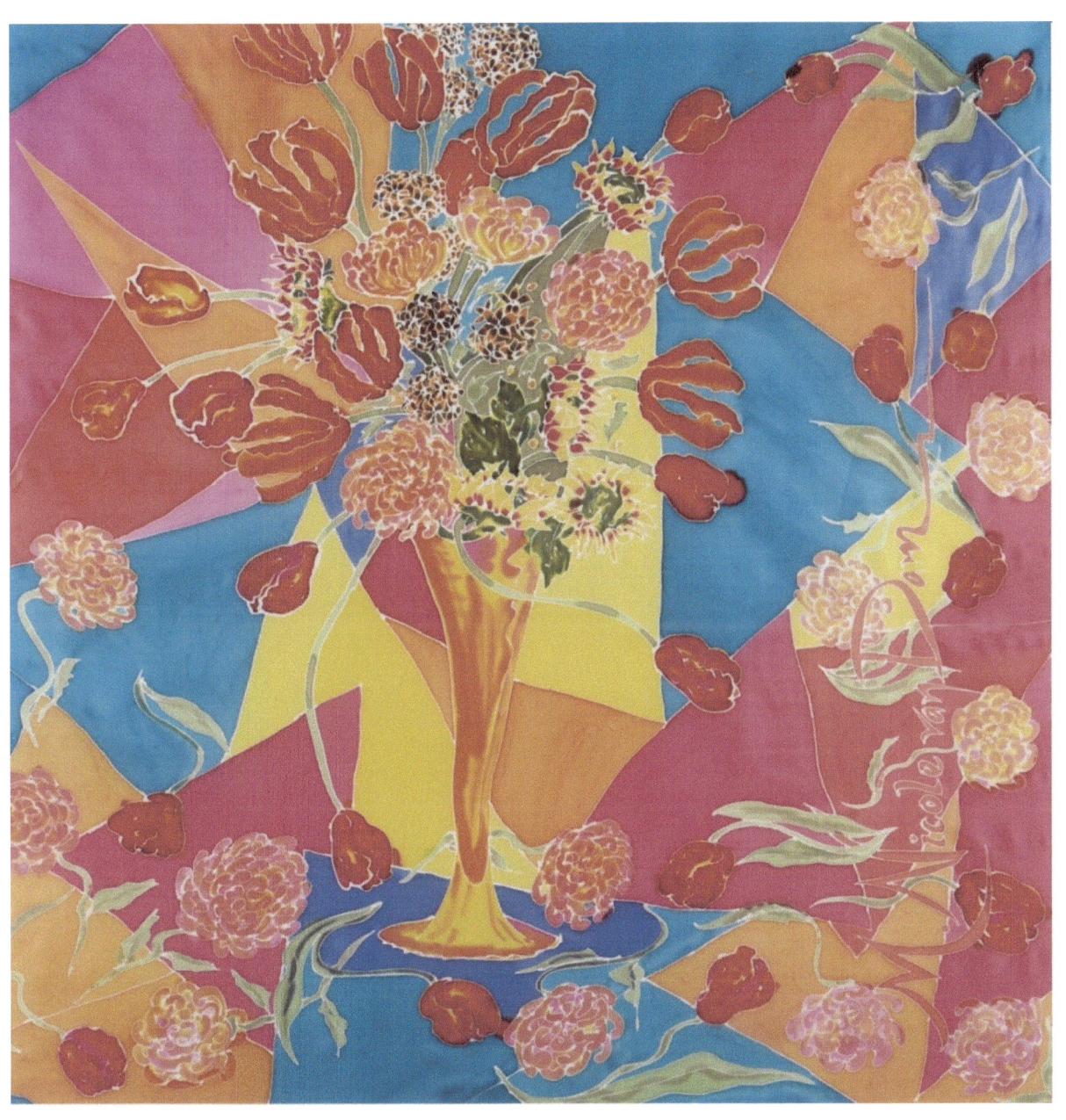

PASSION FLOWER
(1999)

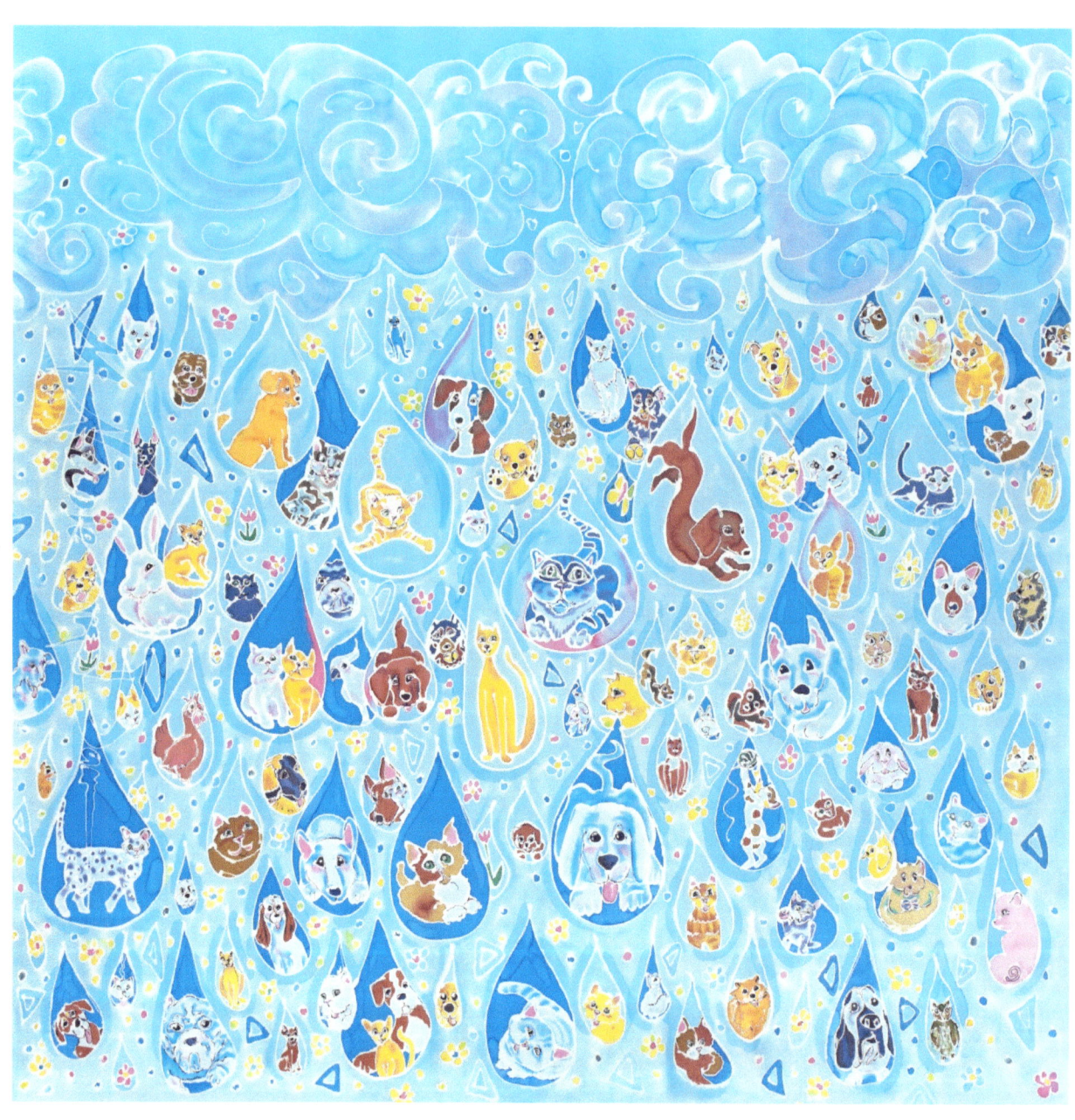

RAINING CATS & DOGS & ...
(2015)

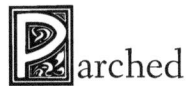arched

When I am in the city

I never hear a plane

My mind drowns out the extra noise

Like my heart drowns out your name

When rain fell ev'ry winter

No drip or drop was heard

My ears didn't measure rain's sound

I didn't treasure your words

Now we're in a long drought

I'm missing the rain almost as much as I miss you

A no lie cloudless sky

My mistakes in clear view

I'm so parched for love

You're the one I'm thinking of

I can't grow without you

Let the torrents of heaven run free

Rain on me

I can't blame you, only me

For my sorry, scorched heart

I didn't forecast all the pain

That comes from being apart

Hope I hear and feel rain again

Hope to be with you too

Miss dancing in rolling thunder

Loving you with all its wonder

I'm so parched for love

You're the one I'm thinking of

I can't grow without you

Let the torrents of heaven run free

Rain on me

Here's wishing you

Missing you

Rain

Rain on me

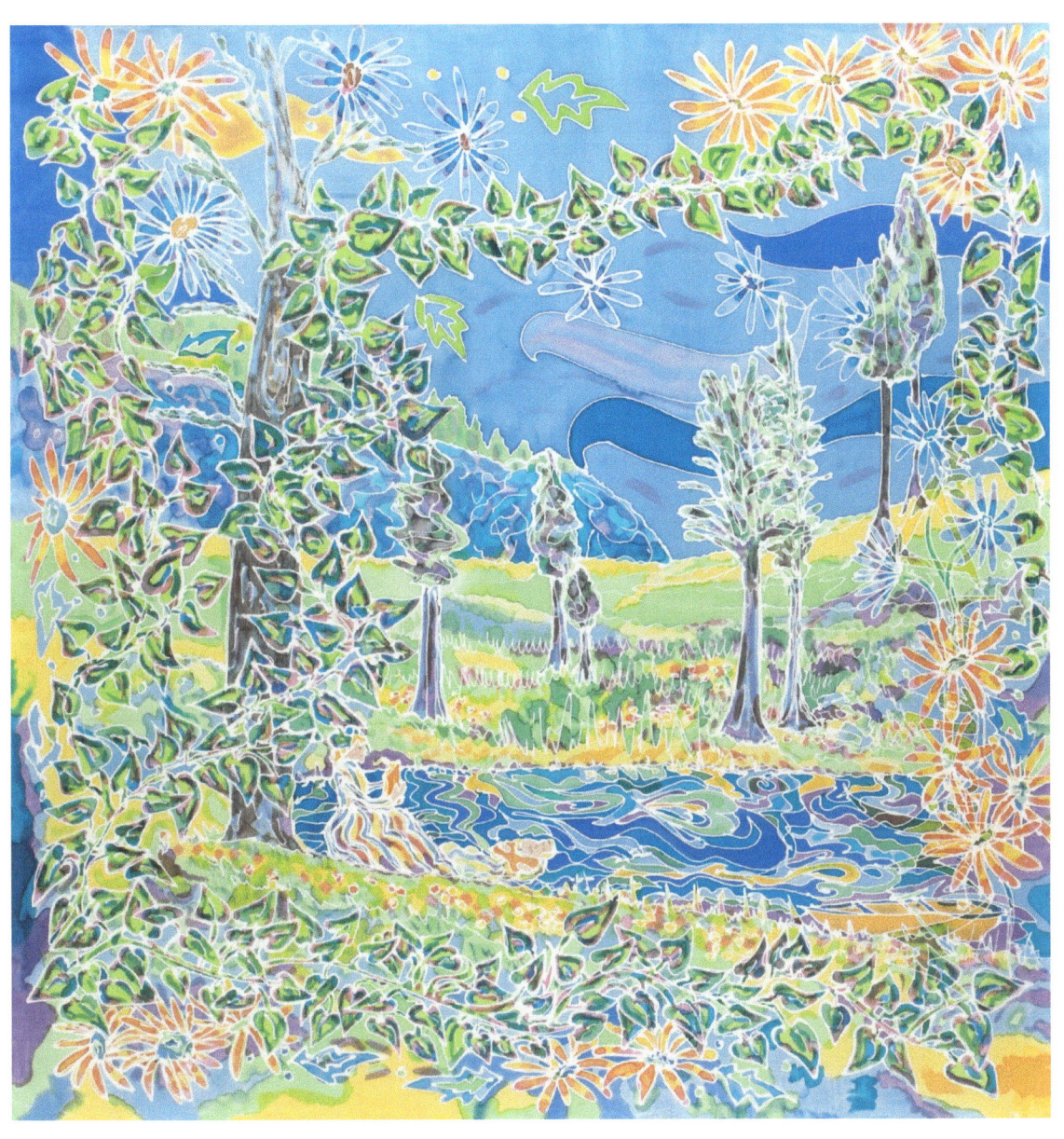

READING ON THE RIVER THALES
(2014)

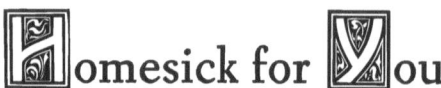Homesick for You

Homesick for you
For what we once shared
Homesick for knowing that someone I really loved and
    admired,
Really cared

Homesick for that feeling of having found my place
Homesick, ever so homesick, for that sunny look on your face
Homesick for just knowing that our love for one another was
    our guide
Homesick for that feeling of safety when I thought I had you by
    my side

Homesick for my little family of two, my best friend
Homesick for that love I thought could never, would never, end
Homesick for a future that never came to be
Homesick for the way the you of you loved the me of me.

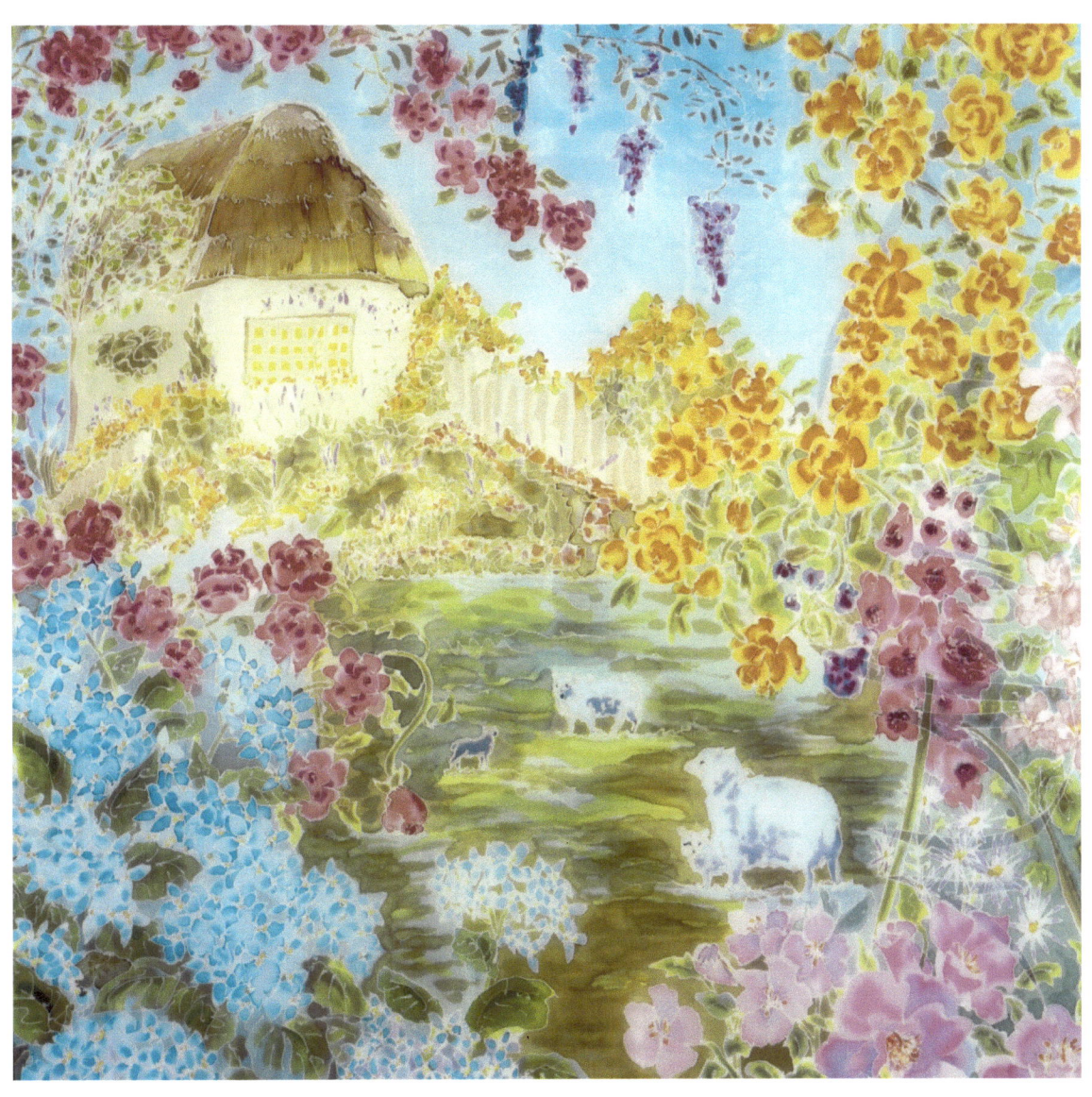

COUNTRY COTTAGE
(2006)

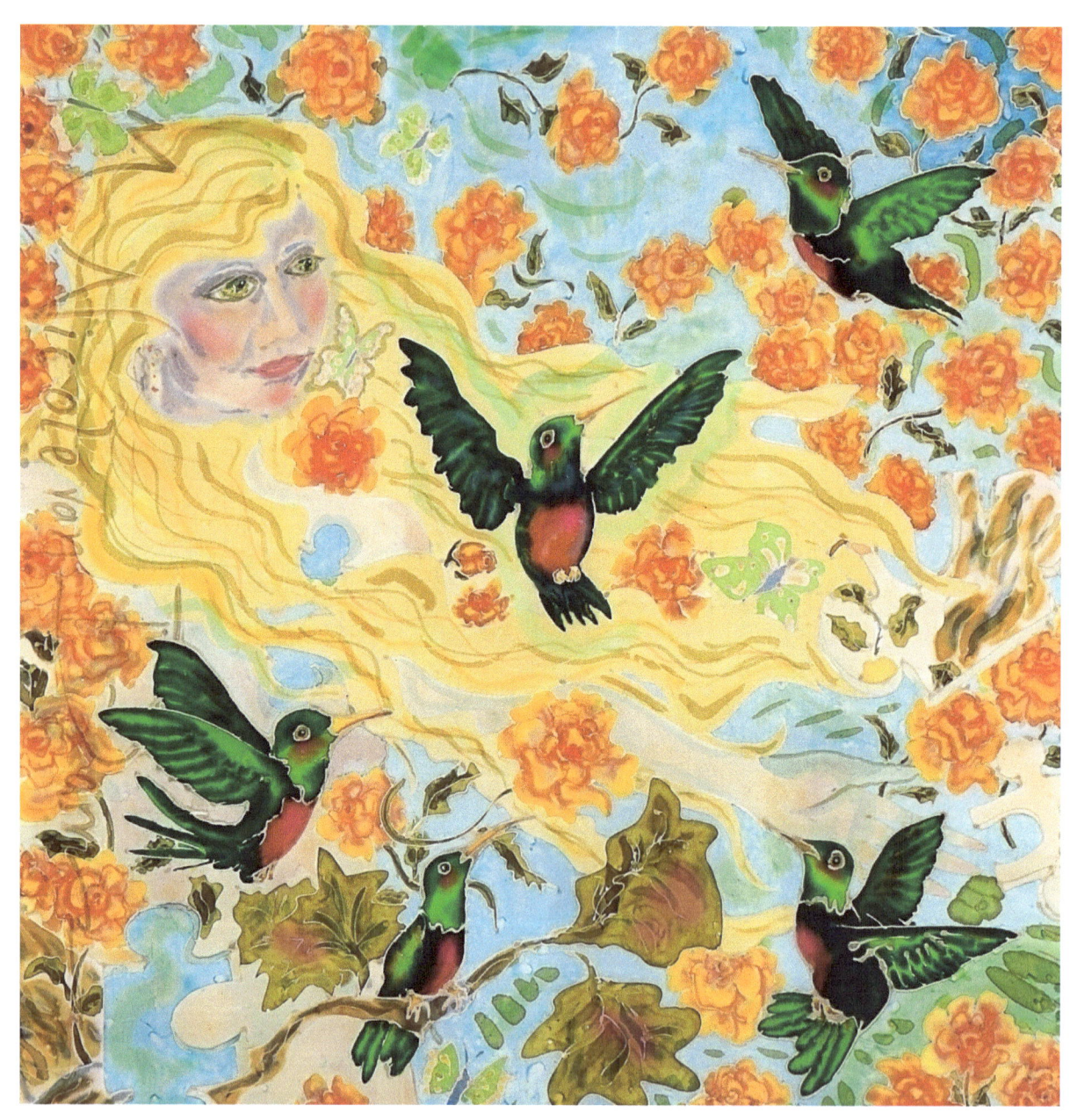

HUMMINGBIRDS AND MISSING PIECES
(2008)

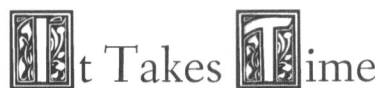It Takes Time

When her ears
Get a little stronger
And she's able to deal
With the man who wronged her

Then she'll listen to gossip about what they said
Her man and that trashy red head
But for now
She needs some time

When her words
Can reach her lips again
And she's able to say
No more breaking my heart my friend

Then she'll make him fess up to the things he's done
Running around loving someone
Telling lies
Being unkind

When her mind
Is a little clearer
And she's able to think
Through the lies he steered her

Then she'll tell him off real good, just you wait
She'll show him out that garden gate
She'll be tough
She'll do just fine

She needs to think it through
What is somebody supposed to do
When the one you love
Breaks your heart in two
She needs time

When her eyes
Can see through all those tears
And she's able to face
All those lost wasted years

Then she'll pick up the pieces of what he's left
Move on quick and try to forget
Beyond pain
Back in the game

When her mouth
Can form words again
And she's able to voice
Being betrayed by her best friend

Then she'll find a way to tell her old dreams goodbye
Find new hopes, give new loves a try
Stay real strong
She will get by

When her heart
Beats a bit steadier
And she's able to face
The truth about who married her

Then she'll pack up her bags and find a better view
Train her heart to love someone new
Make good times
Build a new life

She needs to work it out
See what this world is all about
When the one you love
Breaks your heart in two
It takes time

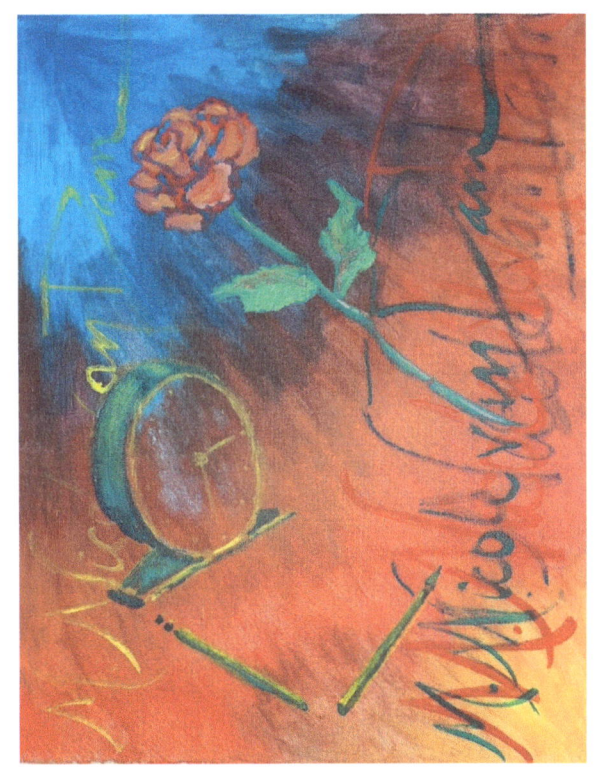

SELF PORTRAIT
(2002)

aper Boats

How you lure me with your paper boats
Sailing swiftly under an insincere sunny sky
How easily I drift your way
Unthinking as to how or why

I believe your false promises so readily
Steering happily into your turbulent seas
Depending without questioning
Upon your steadily unsteady breeze

I know your words lead to the cloudy shores of disappointment
That your smiles mean no more than a frown
Today is the day I become wise, my friend
The risk of capsize is at an end.

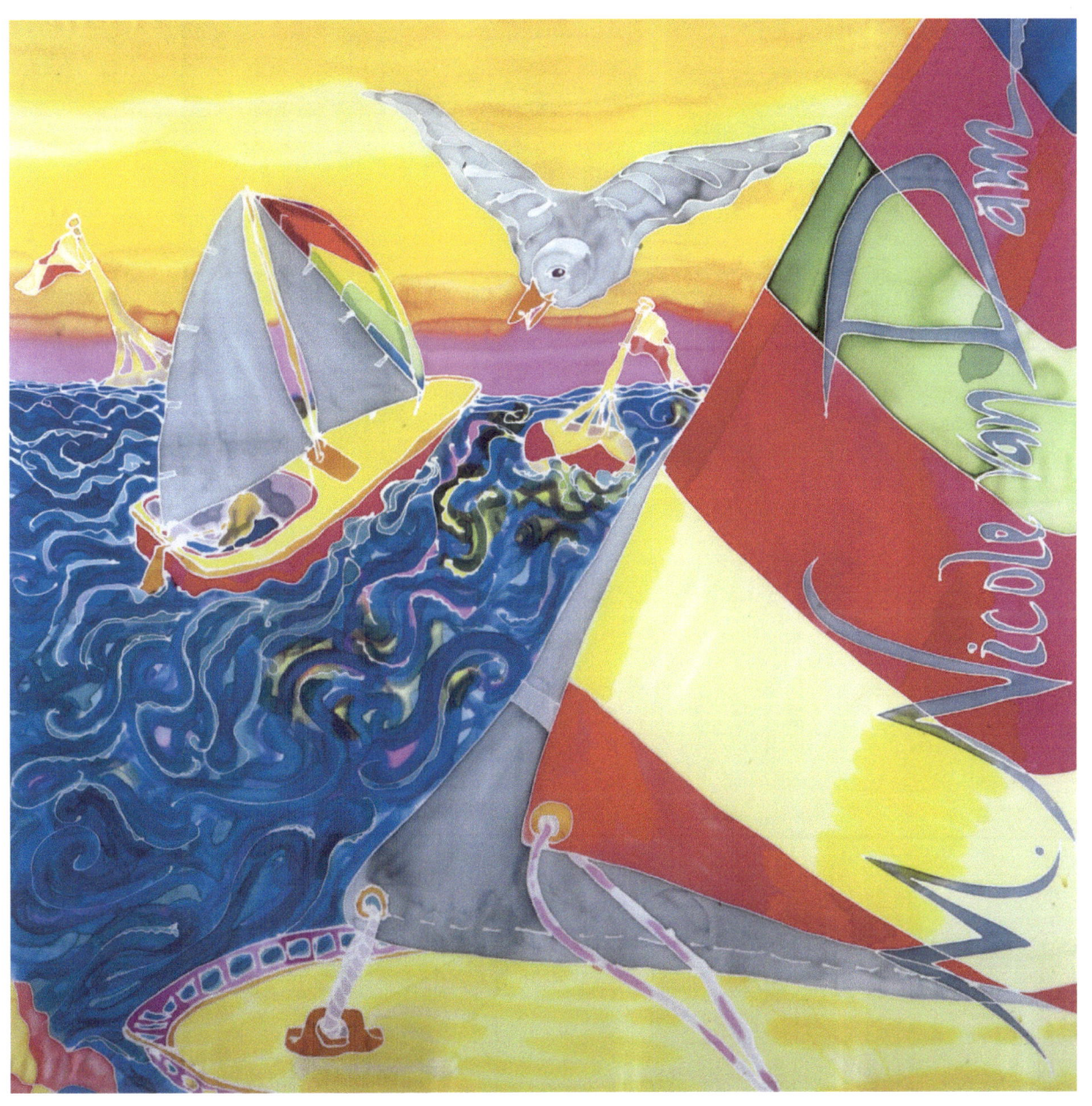

SAILING
(2000)

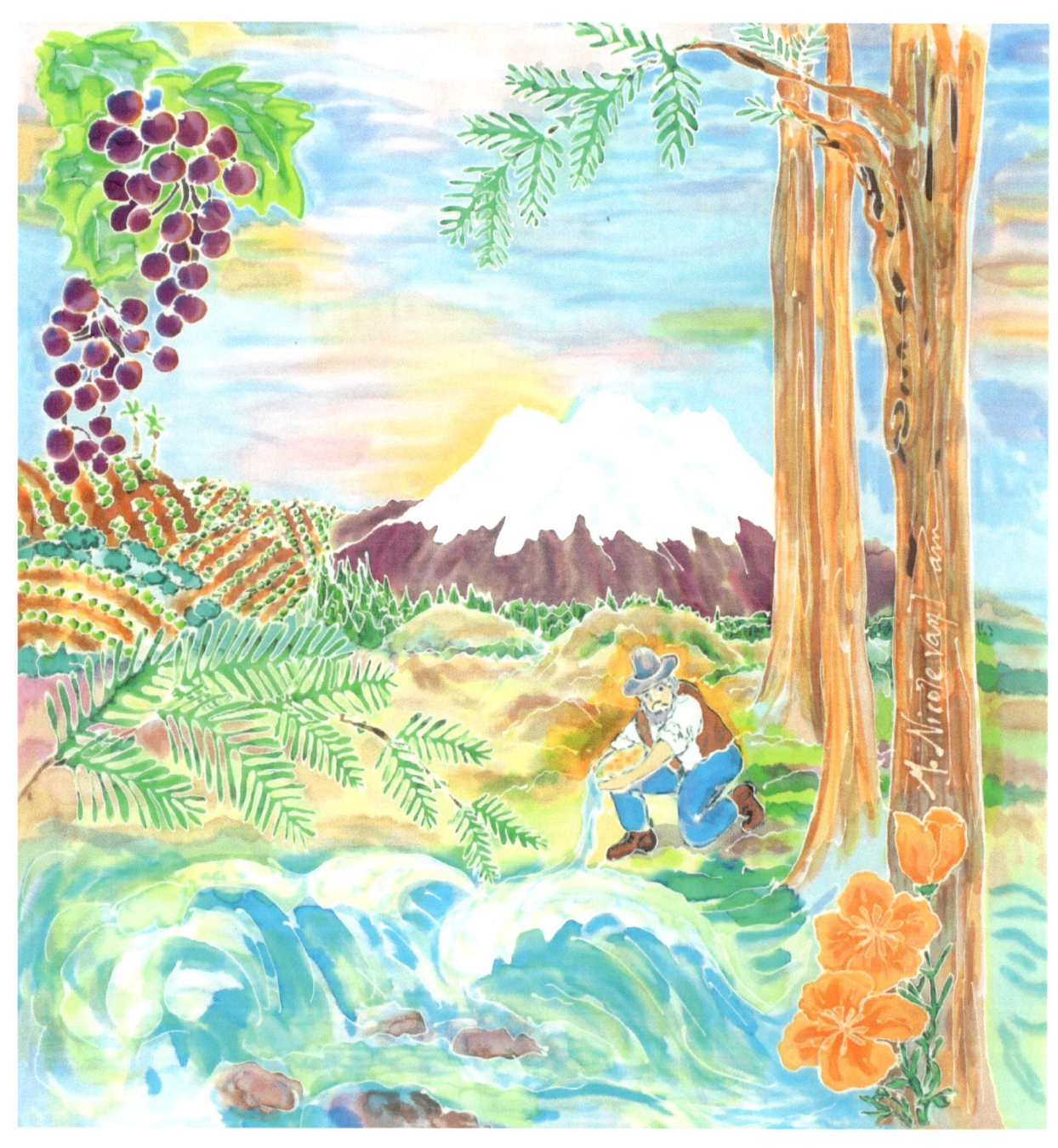

CALIFORNIA GOLD
(2012)

Going Back to the Mines

I'm going back to the mines
Going to find myself a diamond
I'm going back to the mines
Going to find myself a jewel
Going back to the mines
Going to find someone who loves me
I'm nobody's fool

I've been a miner for years now
Looking for love
All I've found is fool's gold
Shiny at first
Tarnished when old

I'm going back to the mines
Going to find myself my one true love
I'm going back to the mines
Going to find the one I'm dreaming of

Going back to the mines
Going to throw you back in
And begin
Again

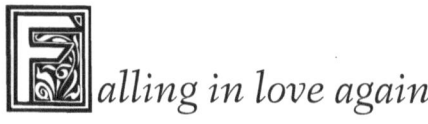*alling in love again*

is the triumph of Optimism over Experience.

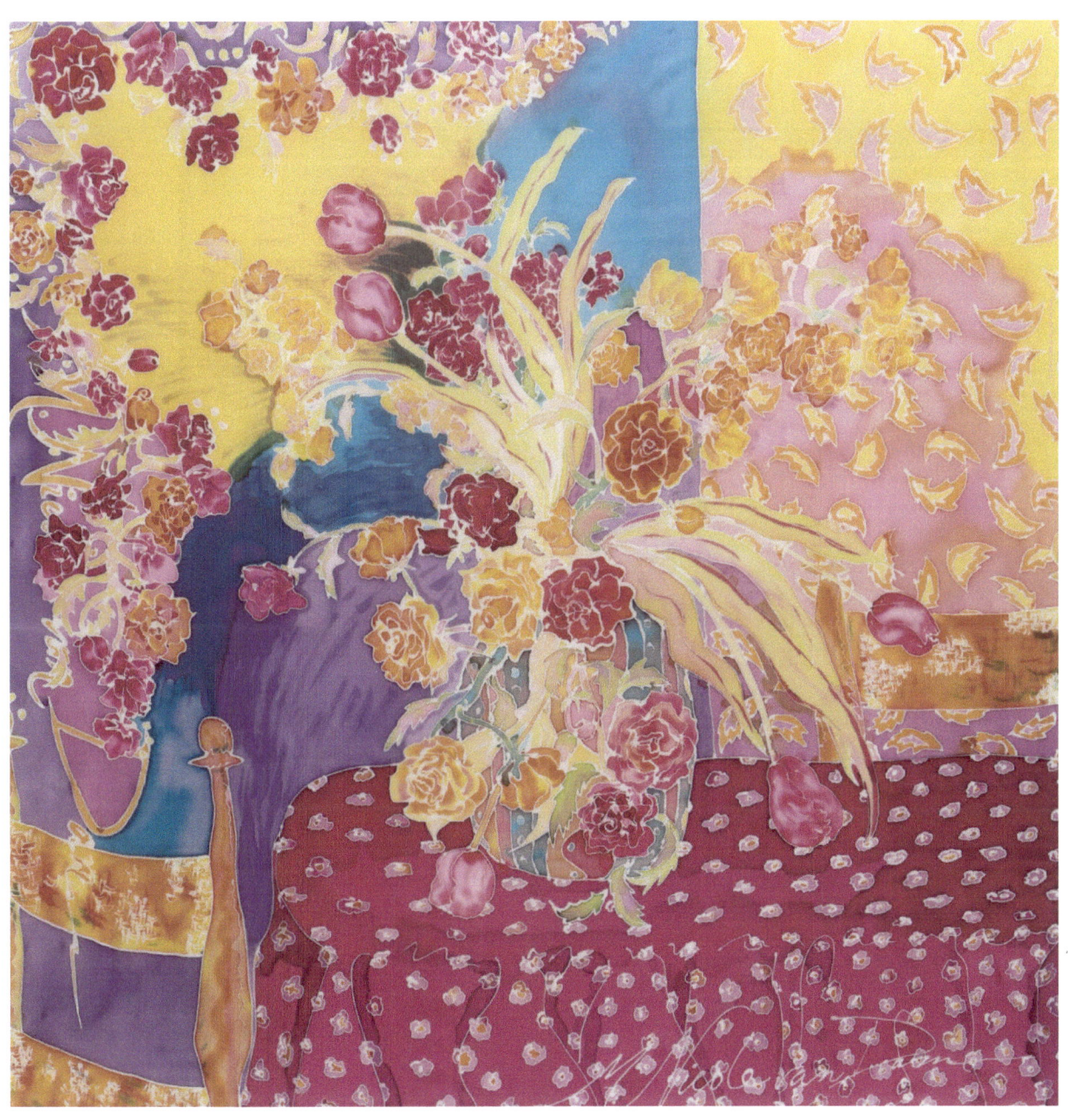

COUNTRY ROSE
(1999)

Nothing soothes

Life's grooves

As a dear, dear friend

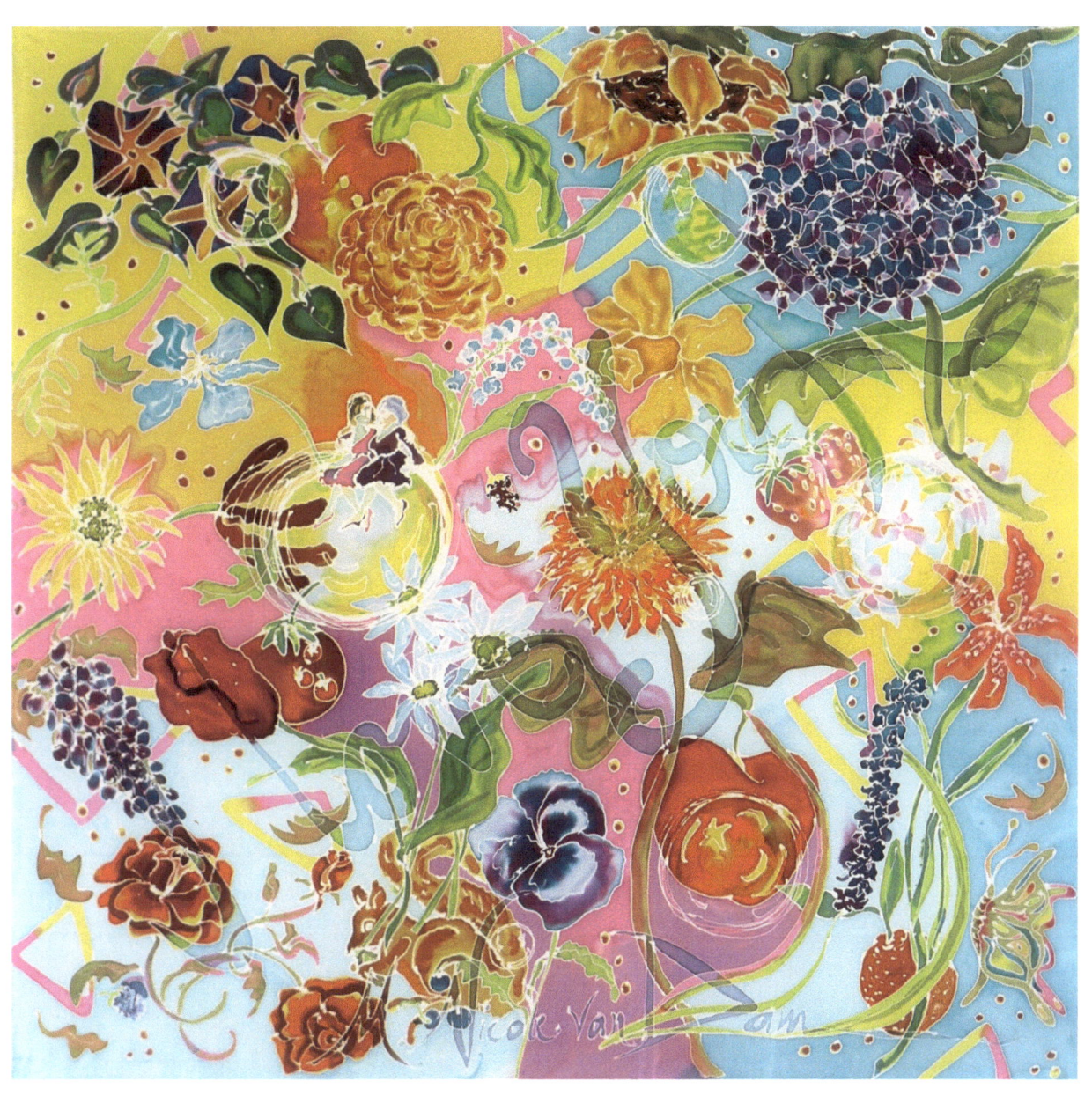

I Love You Mom
(2005)

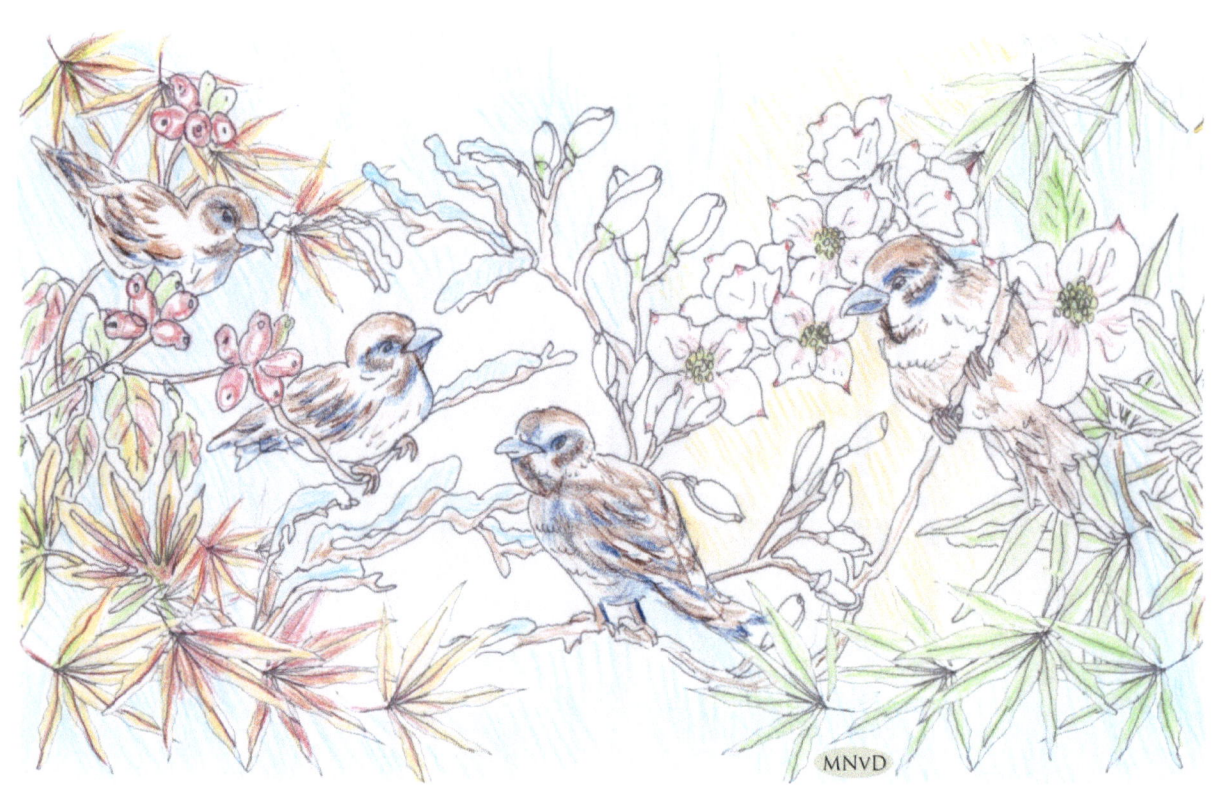

SEASON'S SPARROW
Colored Pencil (2006)

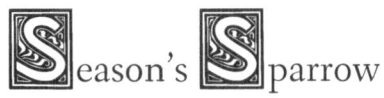eason's Sparrow

Sparrow of Winter
Where did you go
Almost disappearing
Behind drifts of snow
You live in a world of crystal
Glittering ice lining each branch and thistle
Sparkling as you flit your quiet dance
Before you take flight

Sparrow of Spring
In the dogwoods I hear your sweet song
You will be well hidden amidst the leaves
Before long
I see you flying, seeking your mate
Soaring through pastel skies on nature's date
Building your nest amidst blossoms, buds and green
Your nursery soon full and not easily seen

Sparrow of Summer
Awash in a sea of leaves
Happily singing in the lazy breeze
Your job is done, an empty nest
Testifying that you've earned your rest

But 'tis not all chirp and play
As you busily store Summer's abundance
For another day

Sparrow of Autumn
Luminous fluttering falling leaves barely distract your eye
As you curiously watch plain me pass by
Raking leaves

You should know me by now, I think you do
I am the one, rain or shine, to fill your feeder for you
Framed by this world jeweled gold and red
The table is well set for my Sparrow to be fed

My Sparrow of Winter, Spring, Summer and Autumn
My dear, dear friend
I look forward
to spending the seasons with you again.

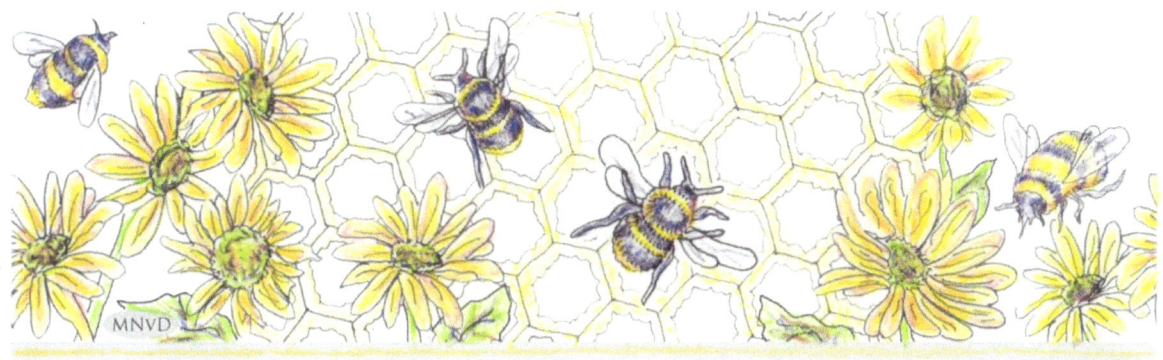

HONEY BEE HAPPY

Colored Pencil (2007)

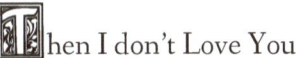hen I don't Love You

If MIT can prove that bumblebees don't fly
And each poor bee, in hearing that, drops from the sky
Then I
don't love you

If there ever comes a day
That rain never hits the ground
That ringing bells make no sound
Then I
don't love you

When day is darker than night
When grass is light blue to all in sight
When every wrong answer becomes right
Then I
don't love you

Undoubtedly sometime soon
When every rose forgets to bloom
When it snows elephants in June
Then and only then
Will I
not
Love You

s an artist, when I am happy, I paint the world in honeydew pastels;

When my heart breaks, it shatters into stained glass.

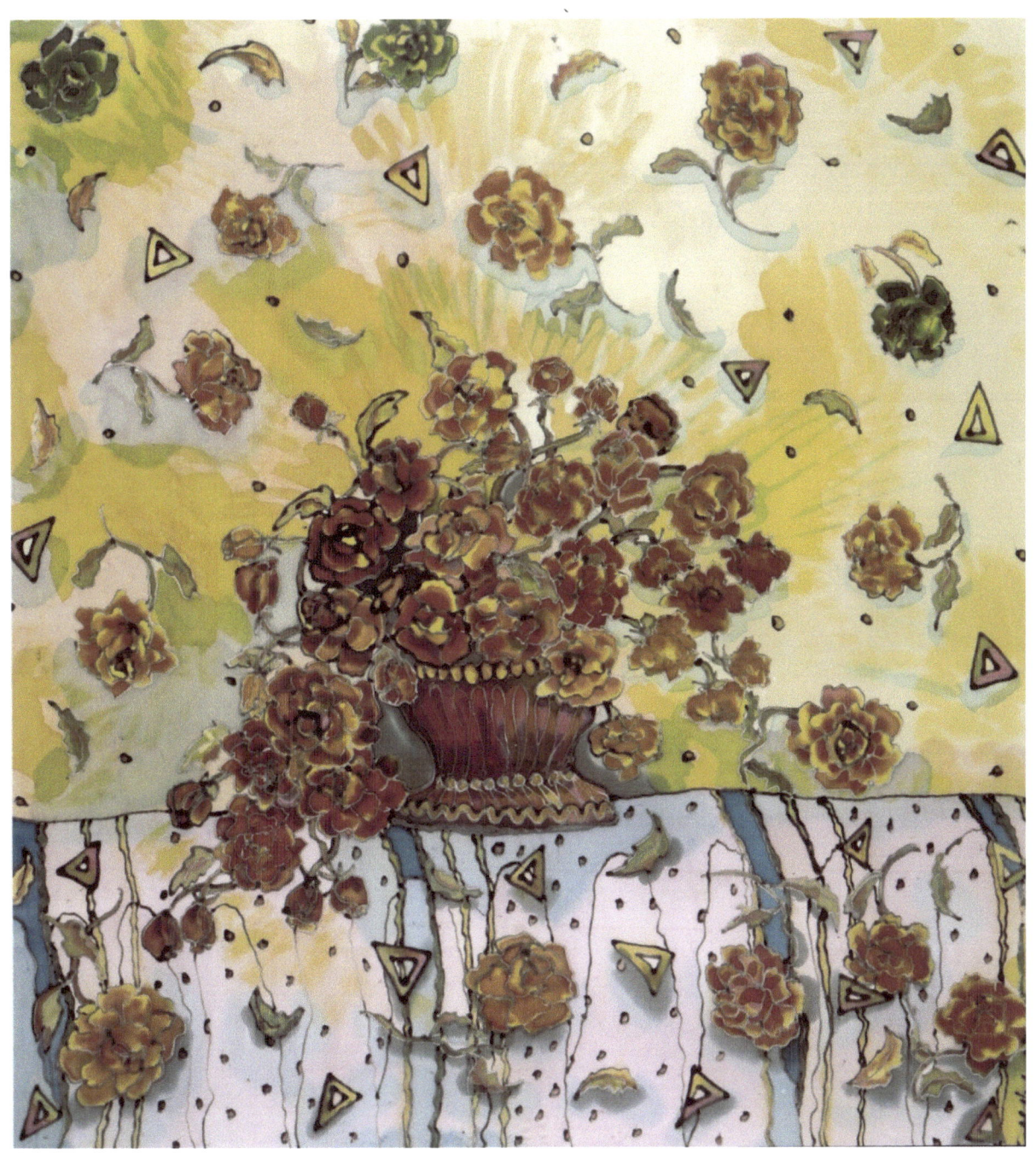

ROSES OF CONQUEST
(2004)

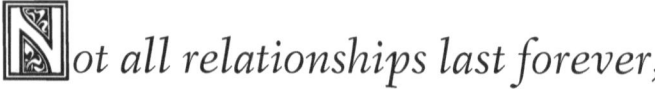ot all relationships last forever,

  but I have discovered that,

Even when I wish a relationship to endure the eons,

  Every relationship lasts exactly as long as it should.

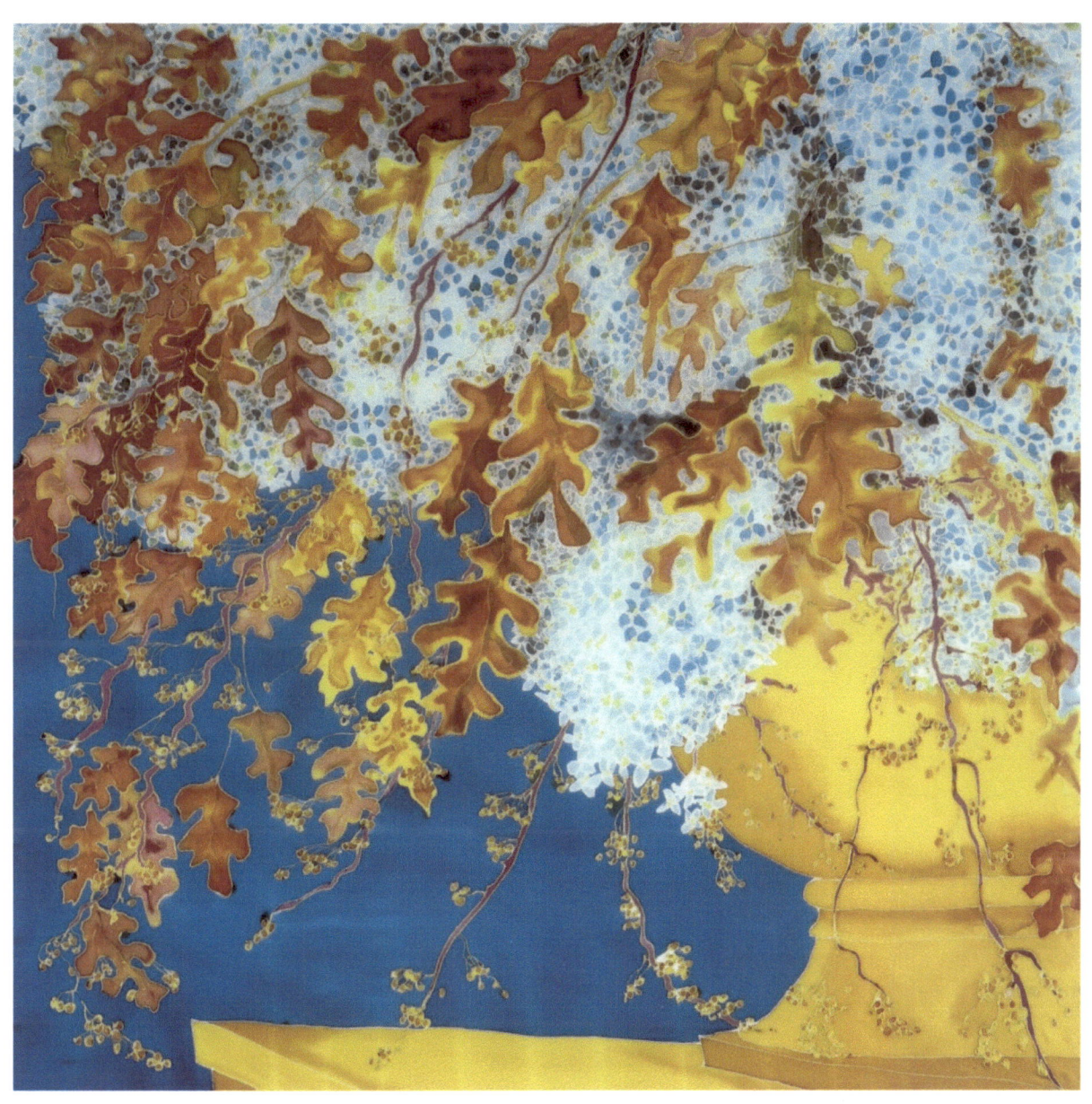

WINTER
(2000)

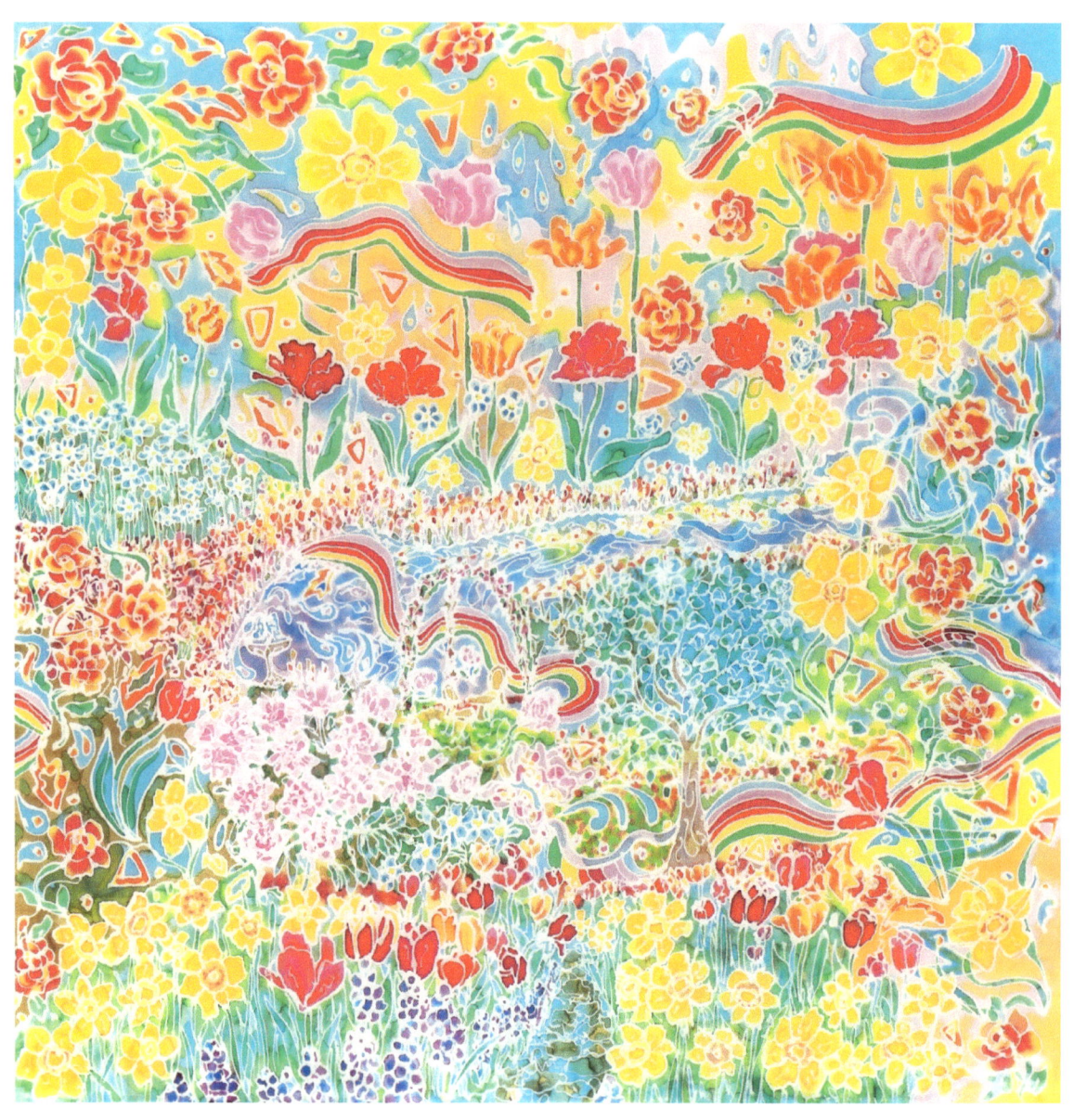

RAINBOW BLOSSOMS
(2014)

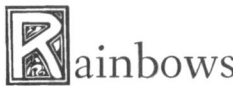ainbows

A Rainbow!
Full of hopes
Full of dreams
Every one knows what a rainbow means
Magic

This moment
Time is paused
Our eyes awed
Colorful beauty takes our breath away
Stand still

Make a wish
One for you
One for me
May our hearts' memory ever see
Rainbows

Adagio

Philosophy

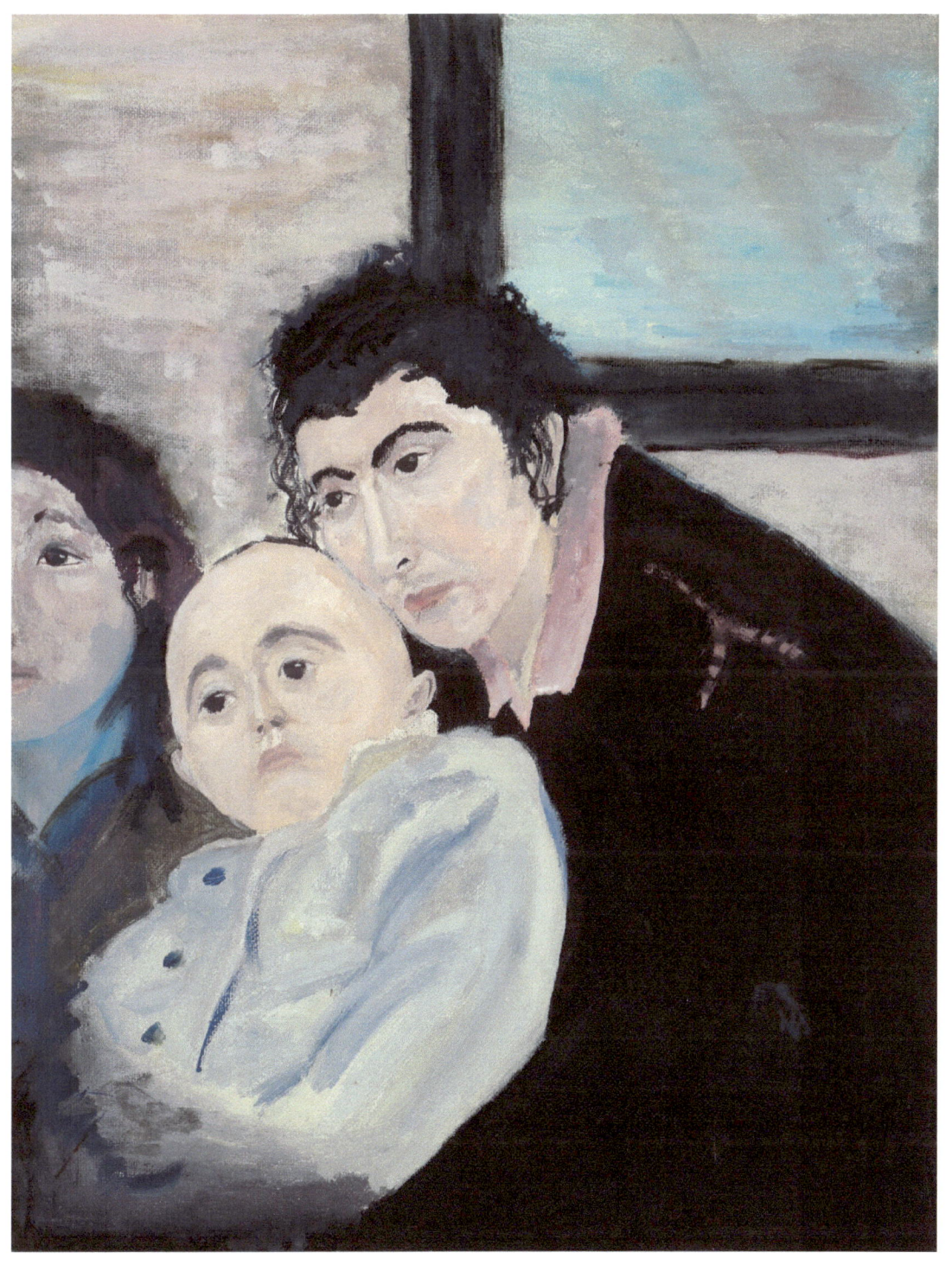

MODERN TRINITY
(1981)

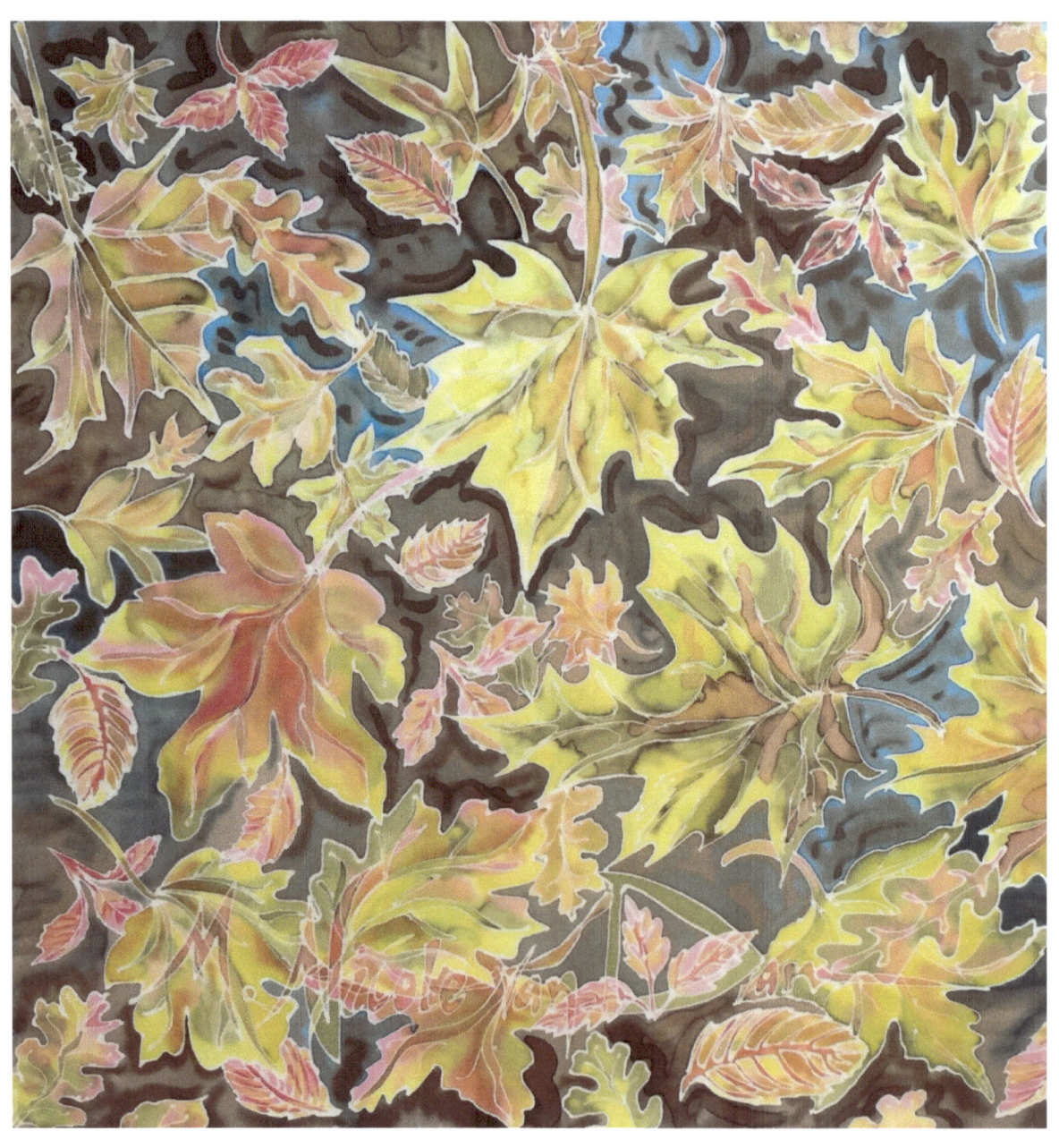

DANCE OF THE FALL LEAVES
(2015)

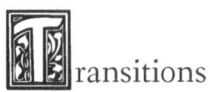ransitions

Each of us is on a mission
To find our life's position
In this large, large world
To find ourselves, test our strengths
To measure who we are by as yet unknown lengths

We find a path
We do well
Or not,
Such is our lot

But know this
Even if we like any of our destiny's trail
Change must prevail
To clutch the status quo
To try to refuse to further go
To deny any route
Is moot
Life inevitably gives us the boot

I've clung to one journey with a death grip
Only to see it easily through my fingers slip
I have learned how much easier it would be
To happily accept that each path is shorter than we foresee
To embrace
With eager grace
Change at a defying pace

To willingly burst upon each journey new
Young at heart, fresh as dew
Soaking in the lessons at each experience's door
And at each chance seeking even more

More life
More love
More laughter
More lessons

There is nothing to be gained
No glory to be retained
By dully walking the self-same worn path
The growth, the joy
Comes from challenging life's decoy
From looking far and near
For the next treasured moment dear
From trying new things
Even if it adds a few more dings
to our delicate souls
Because

At the end of the day
The only dismay
is to choose survival over growth as the way

Don't cling to the past

using "I don't know what to do" as an excuse to make inertia last

Any choice is better than none

Only by *doing* will anything get done

Unfulfilled promise is a life that is sleeping

Truly living's recipe requires action not safe keeping

Don't give in to monotonous days

or to the "what will the neighbors think" craze

Instead: Give yourself a chance to self amaze

Enjoy the journey but

don't expect

don't want

don't try

To make any path last forever

To believe that your life consists of one endless pre-planned endeavor

Transition, transition, transition

Is our only true life's position

Transition is the only path mankind

is certain to find

Embracing change is then the only rule

Our heart, mind and soul our journey's most precious jewel

and our spirit, our attitude, our fate's fuel.

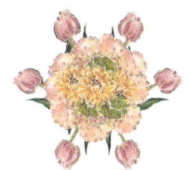

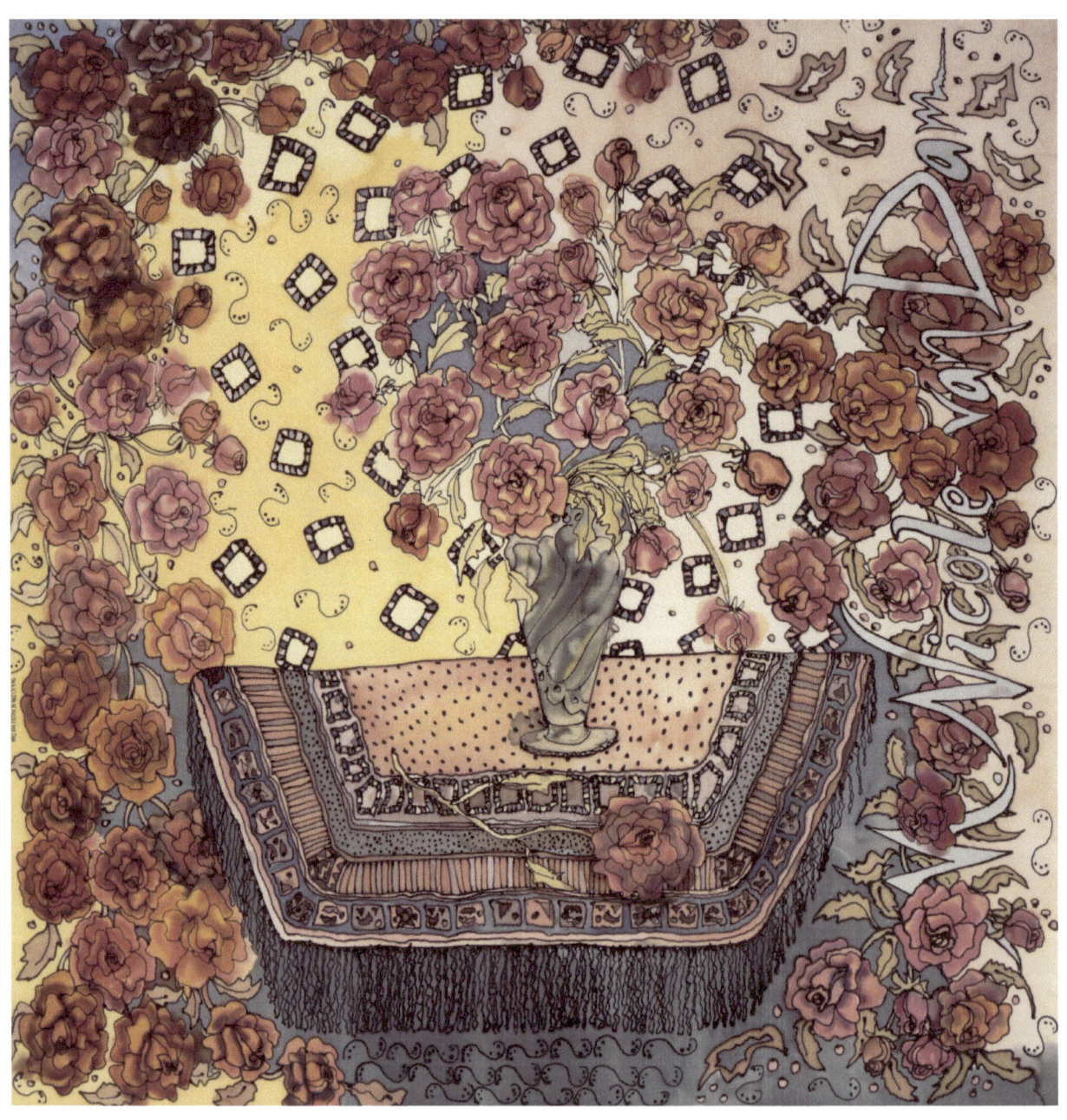

AUTUMN ROSE
(2000)

It takes courage to take responsibility

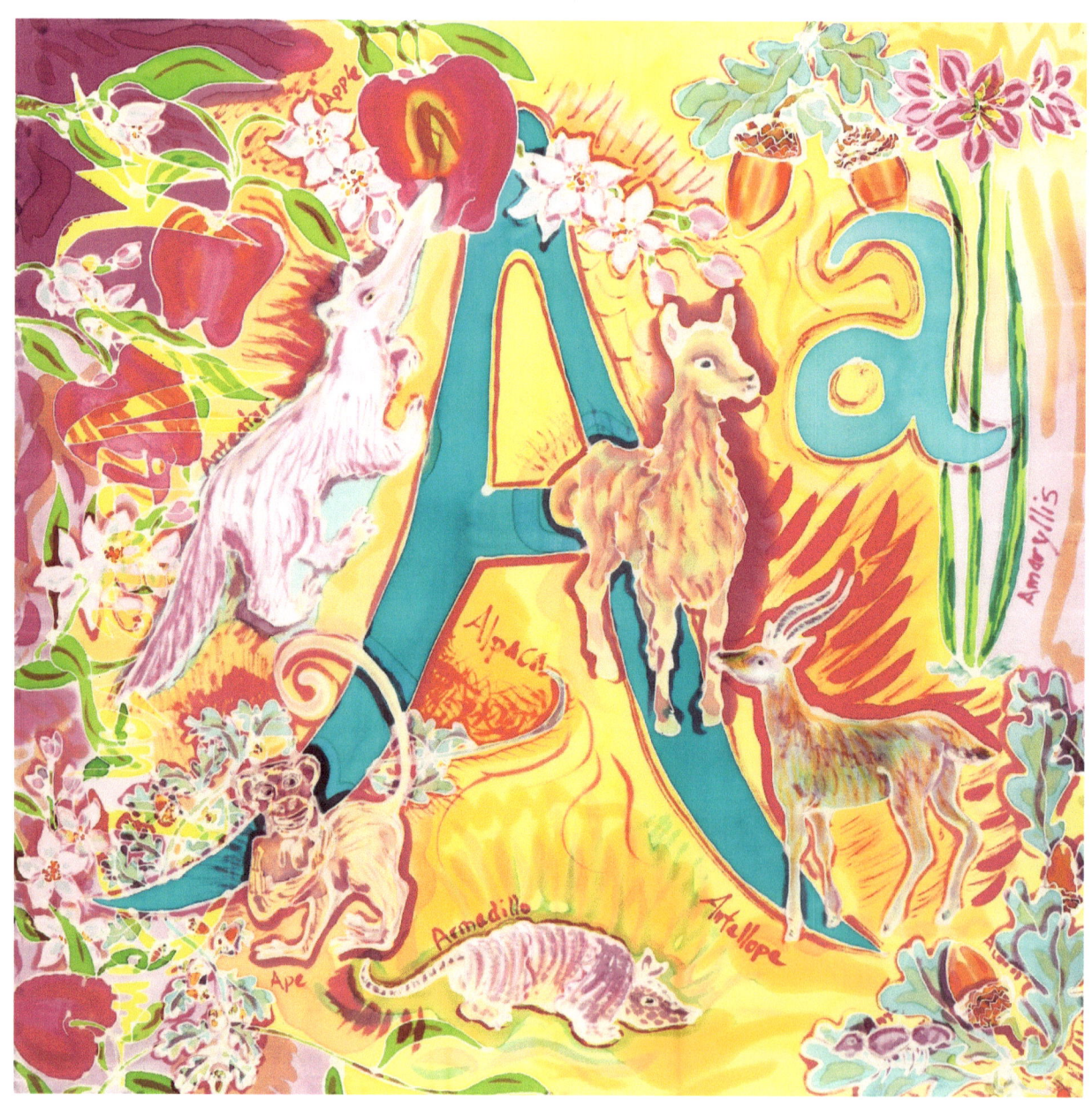

THE LETTER 'A'
(2007)

The best antidote for depression
Is to give your brain the treat
Of learning something new.

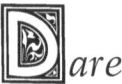are

Don't let your past own today

Don't sell today for the morrow

Don't mortgage your future

Pine not for a past only borrowed

Don't fear laughing, loving or living

Never forget the joy of sharing, caring and giving

Fear not the sorrow of loss

of a soul tempest tossed

Live fully

Set the you of you free

to strive, to shine

Be all that you dare to be.

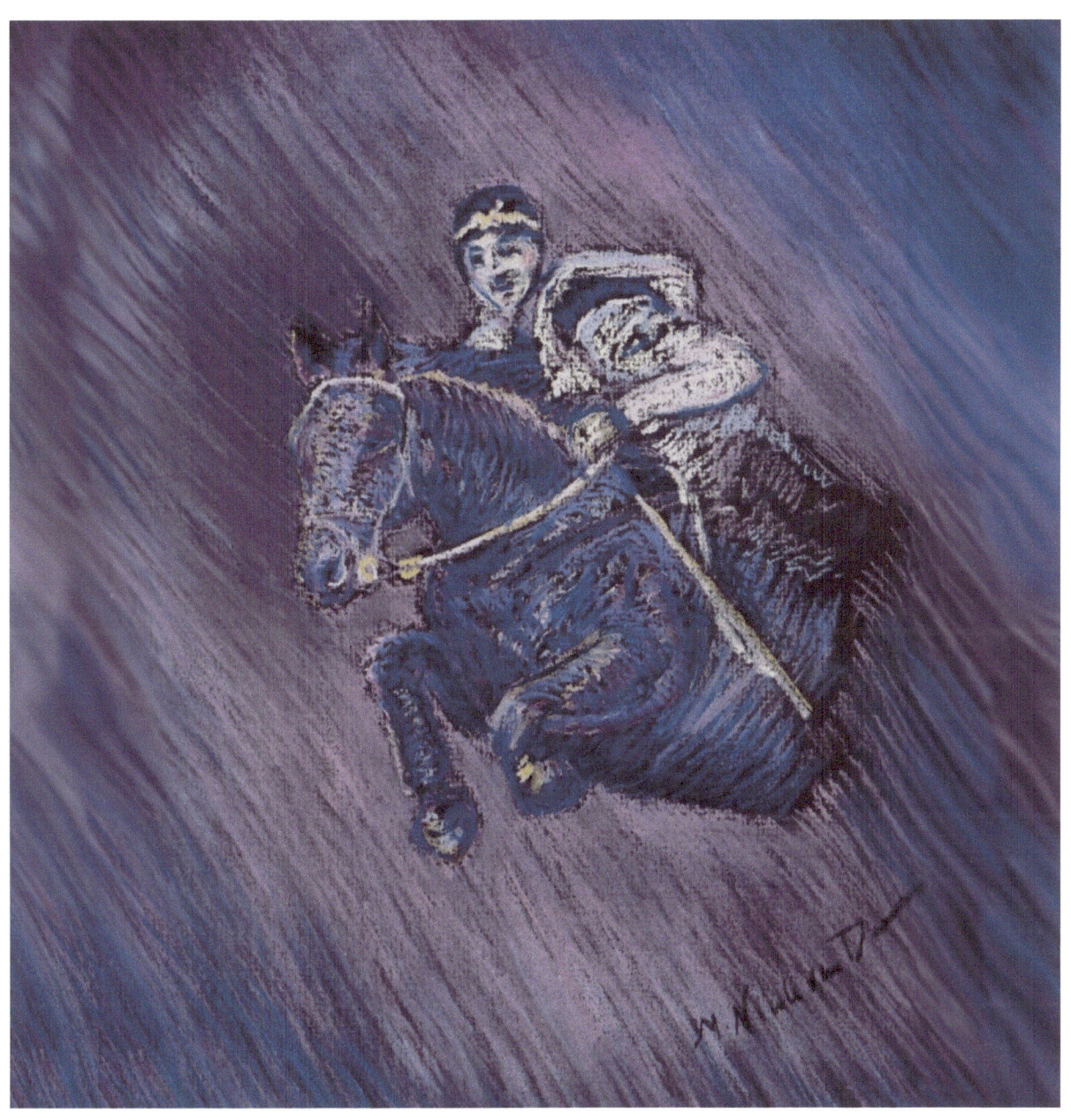

LEAP OF FAITH
Pastel (1995)

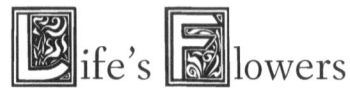ife's Flowers

Why is it so hard to stop the world from spinning
Why can't I cease time while I am winning
Why must the clock tick on and on
Til some end marked by an alarmingly arbitrary gong?

Why can't this moment, for me, of love, hope and joy
Last and last
Why must these jeweled days ever pass?
I love my mate, my folks, friends, dog and cat
I want my life dearly held where it's at

I don't want to lose any of them
I don't want to face loss again
I want to stop the march of age,
The race of hours
NOW
Before another precious petal falls
From my bouquet of life's flowers.

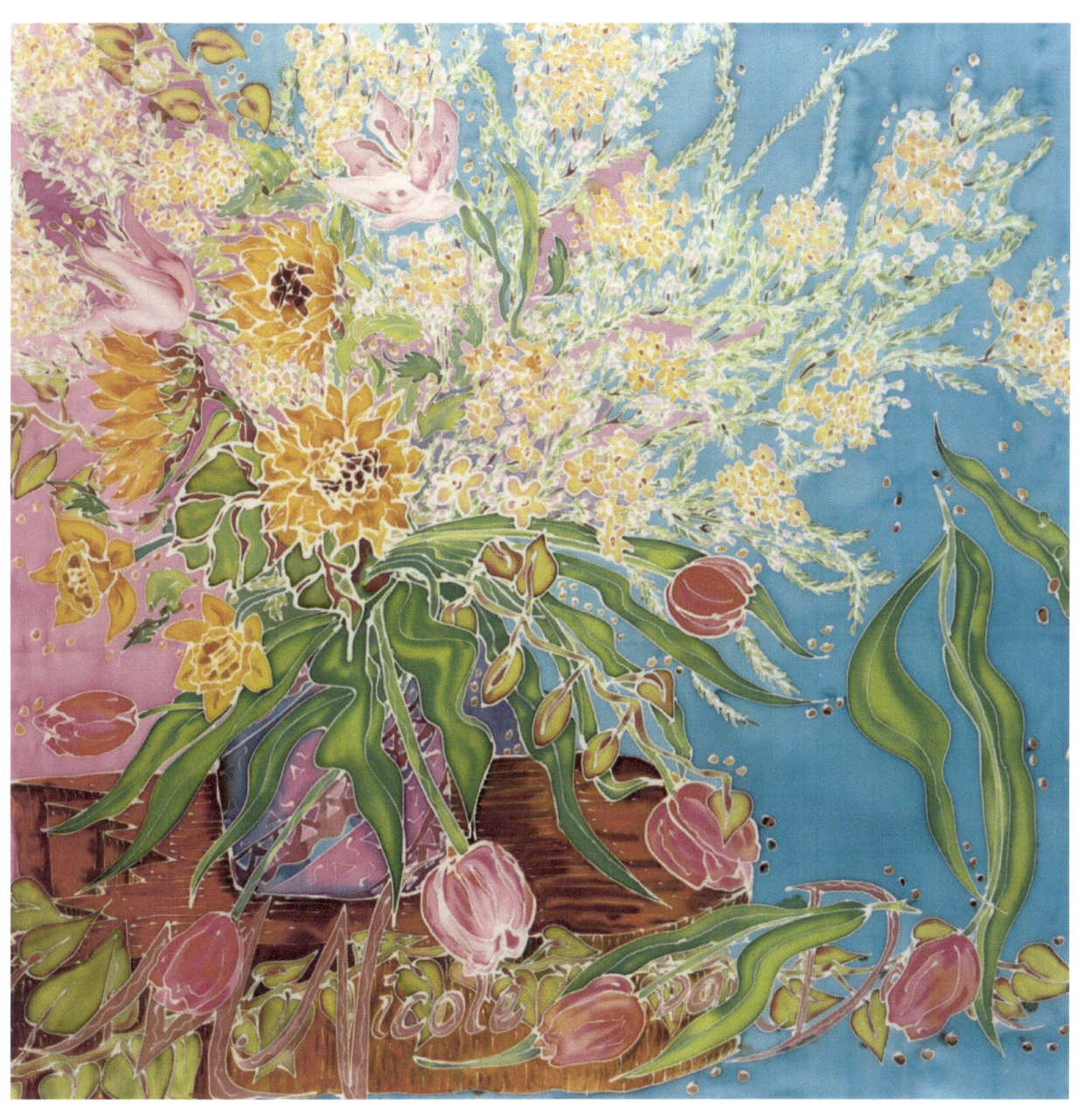

IT'S SPRING
(1999)

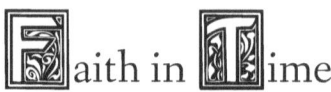aith in Time

The Universe brings you what you are supposed to get

And though more often than not,

I fret

That it's not what I want

Not what I wish

Not that which makes my heart soar

With patience

Open-mindedness

Open heart

I see, in time,

that the Universe gave me much more.

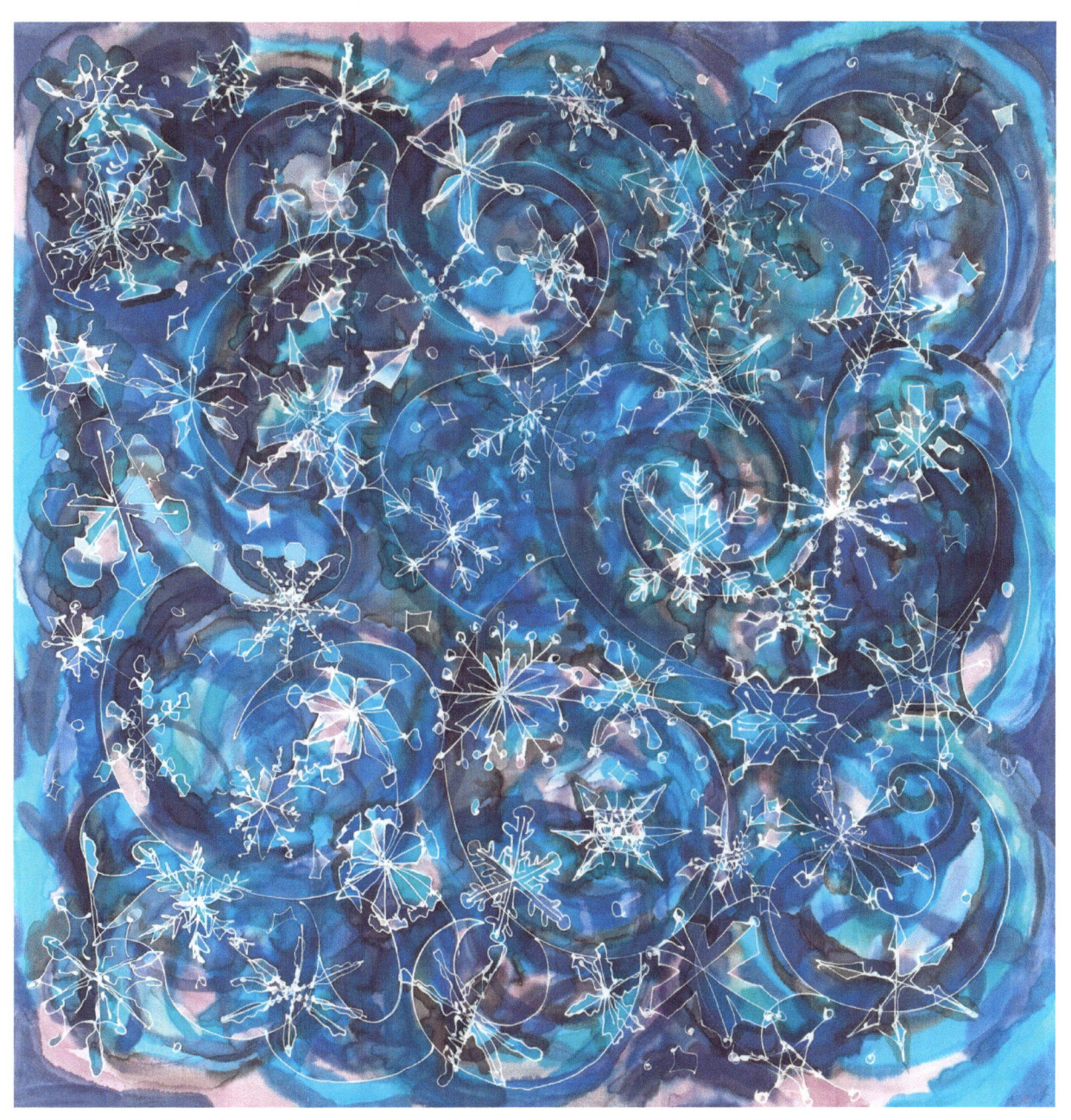

SNOWFLAKE SONATA
(2015)

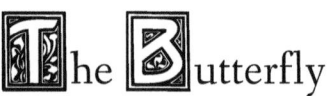

The Butterfly

Frolicking upon flowery pillows

Dancing in the wind

The Papillon in its hither, thither, flit and play

Paints color for our paisley day

If only we look his way.

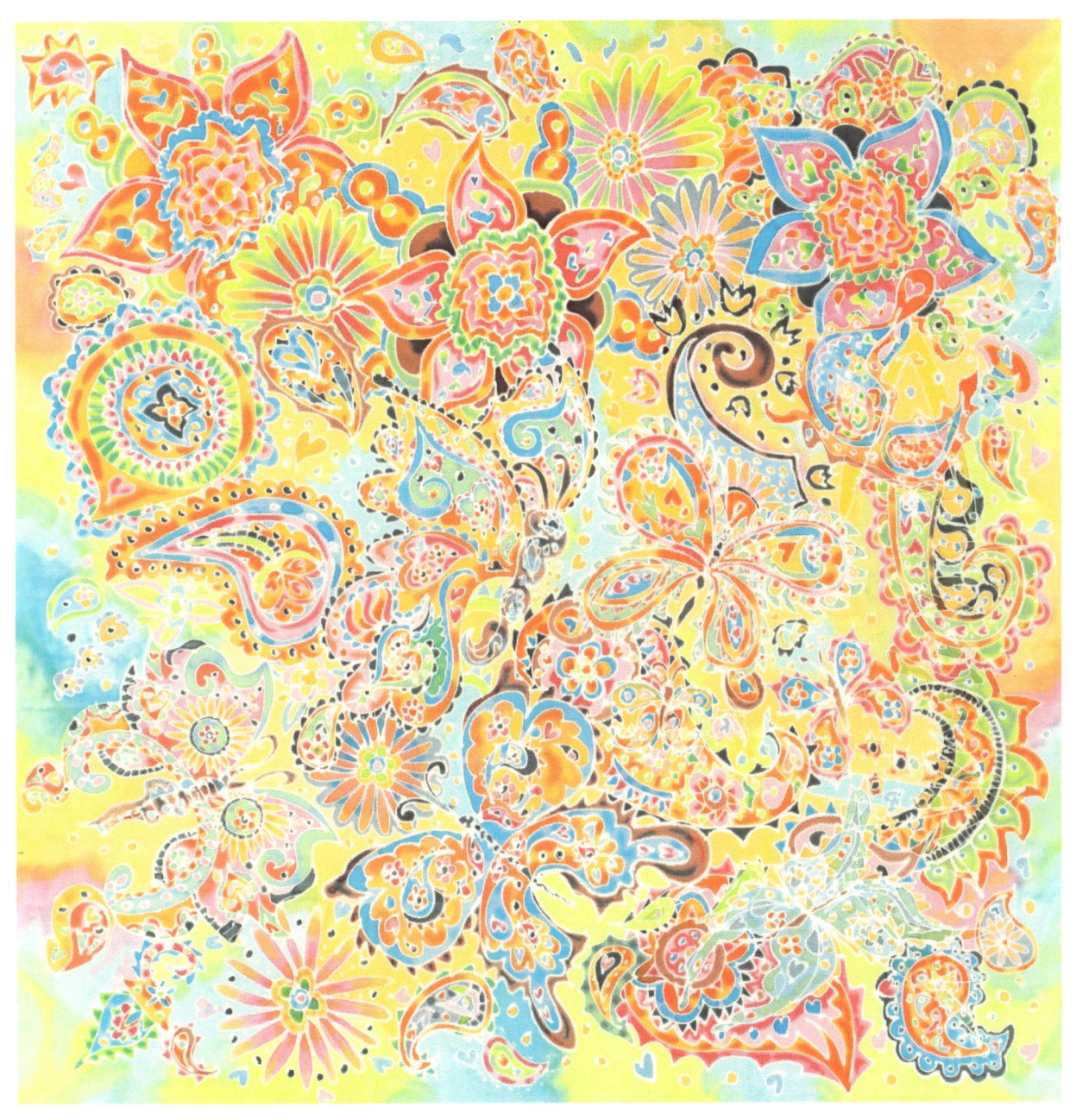

PAPILLONS DE PAISLEY
(2015)

We all paint our worlds, but some of us more knowingly claim our brushes.

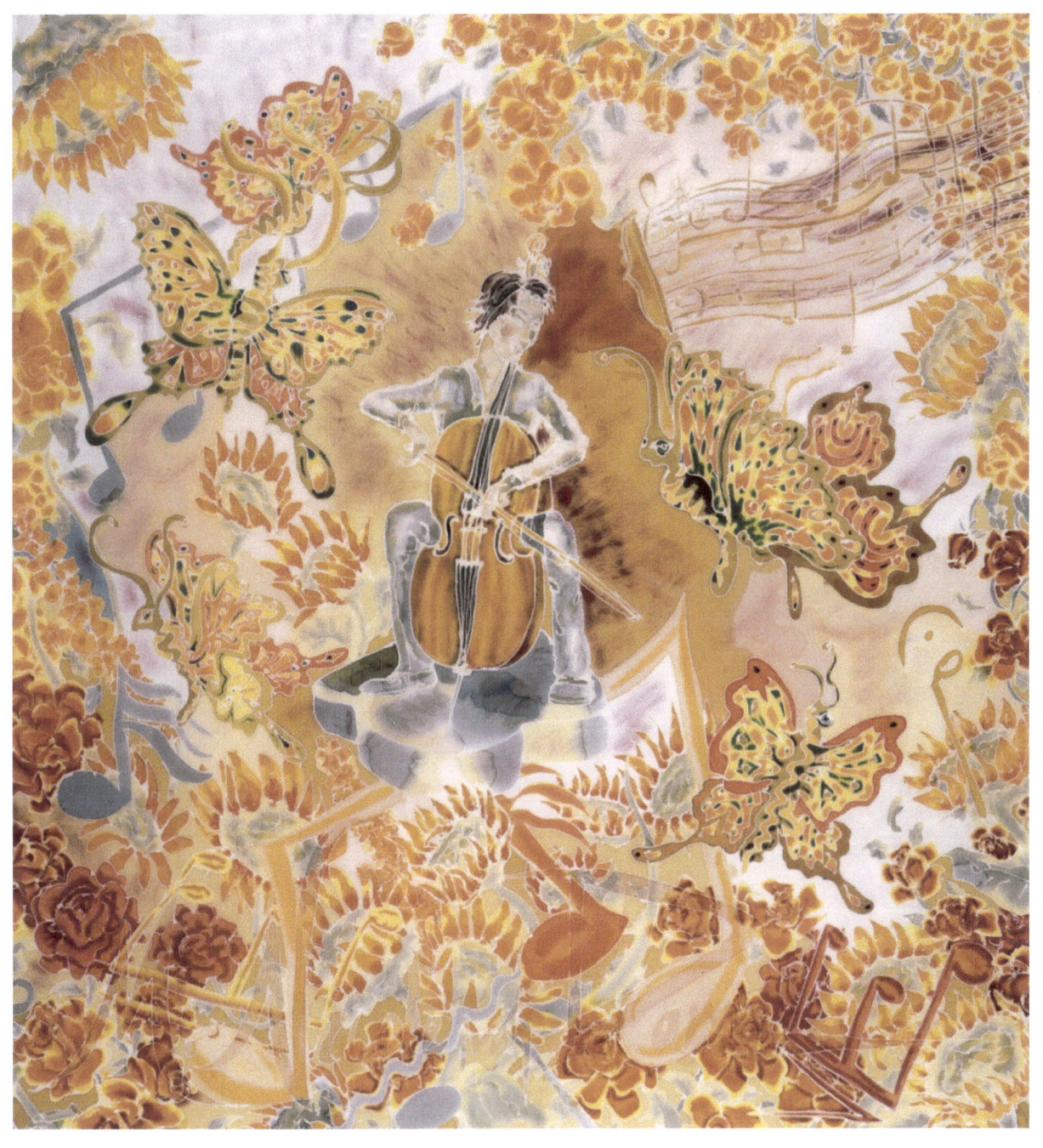

CELLO FANTASY
(2005)

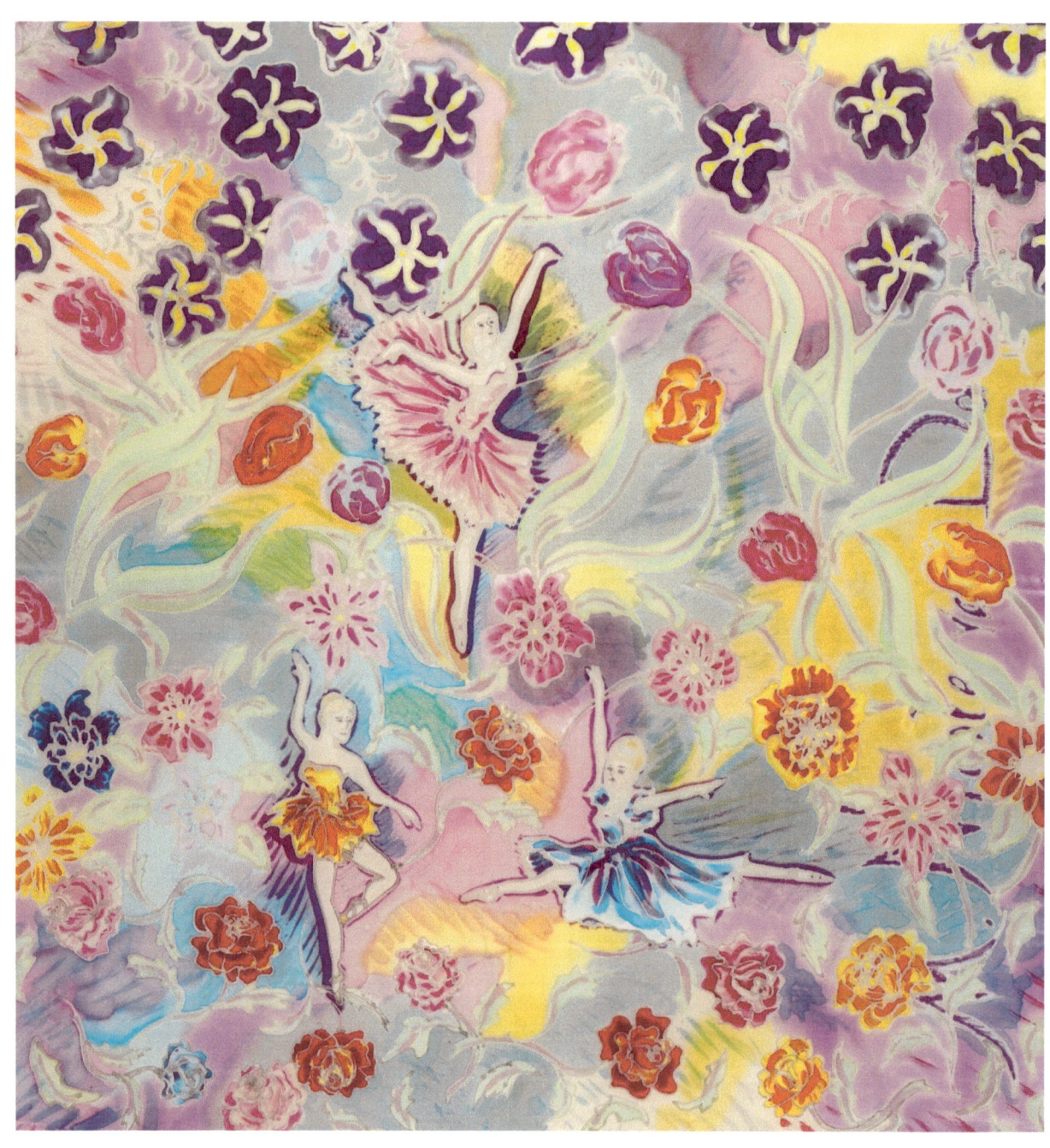

BALLET DES FLEURS
(2007)

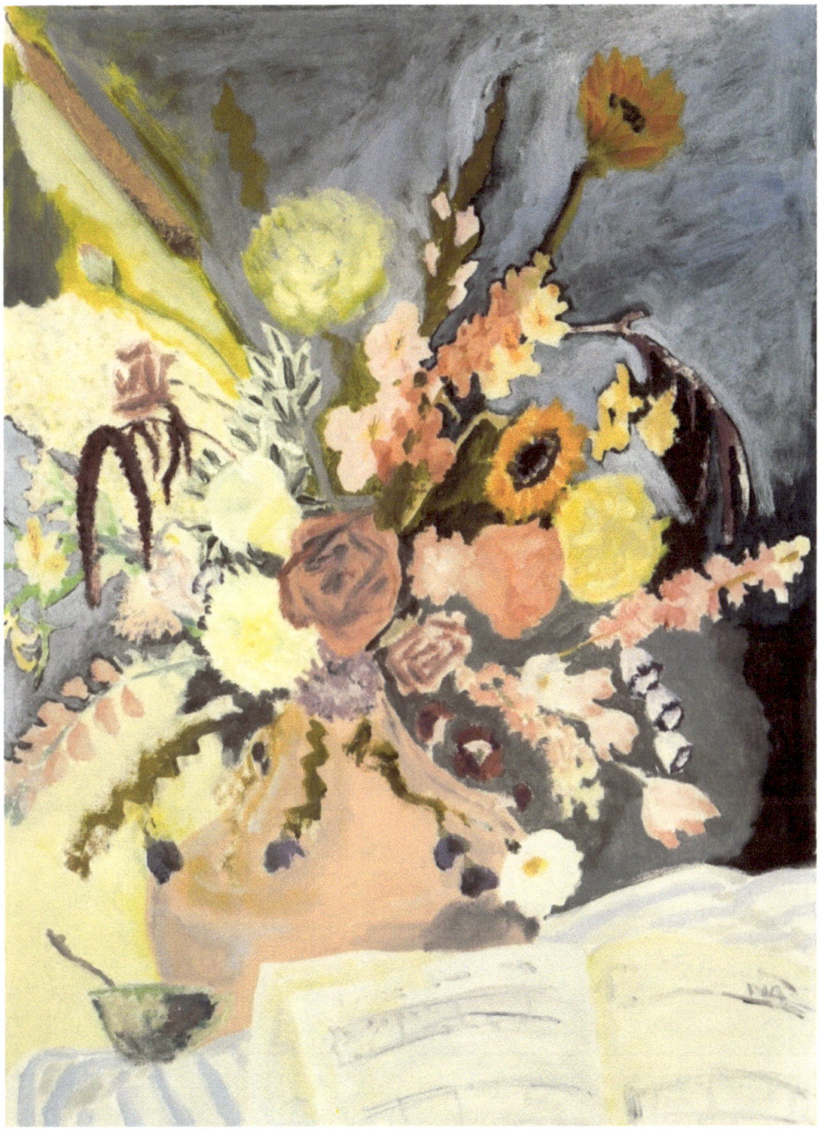

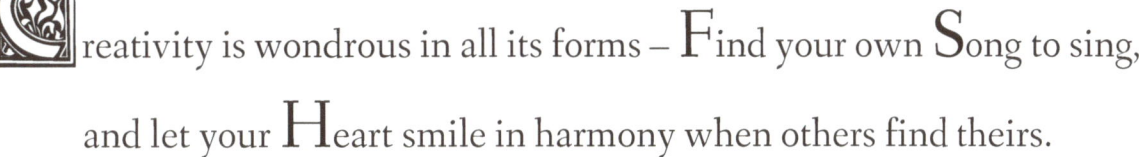

FLOWERS & SONG
Acrylic (1993)

Creativity is wondrous in all its forms – Find your own Song to sing,

and let your Heart smile in harmony when others find theirs.

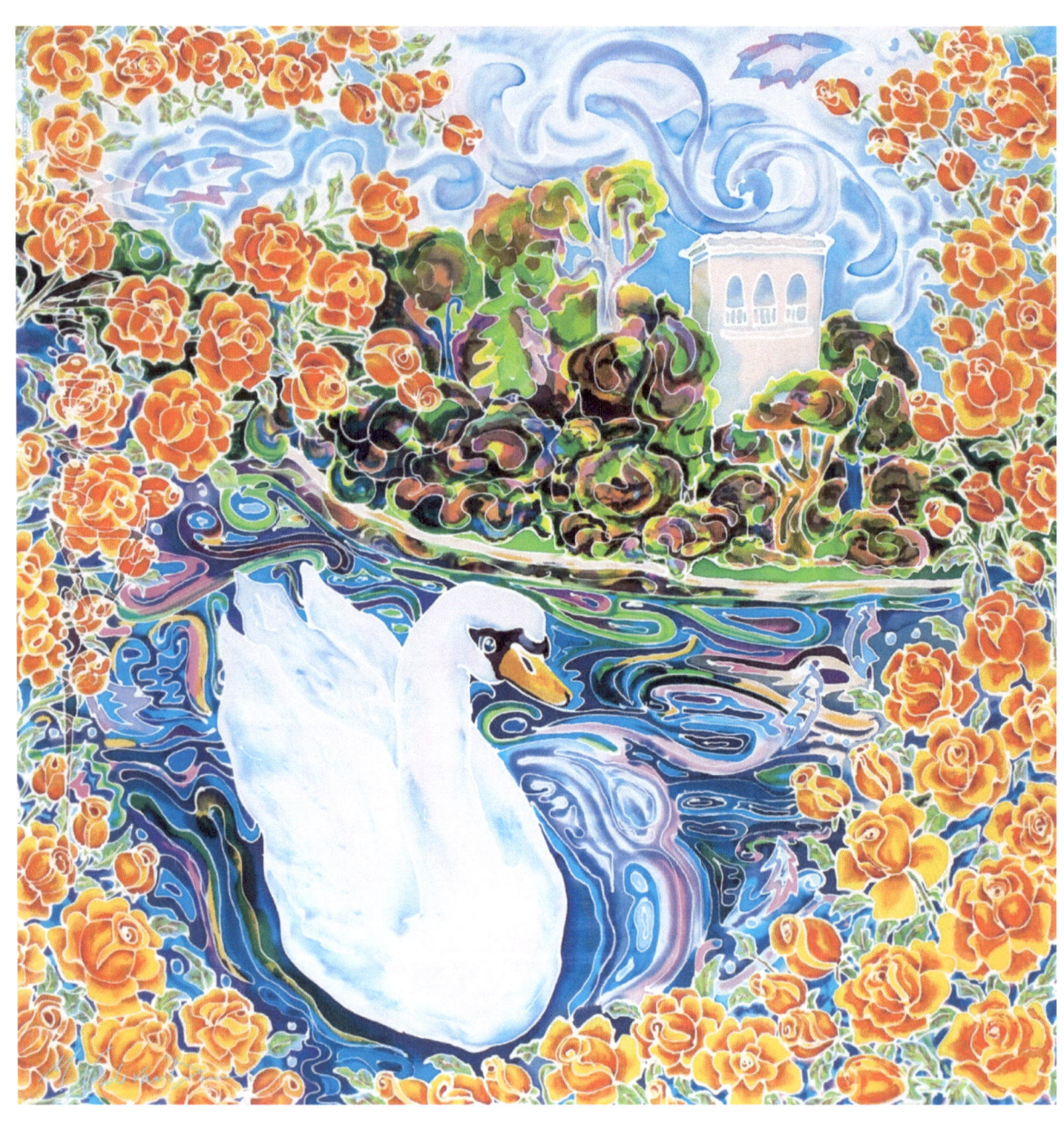

Le Lac de Reves (Lakee of Dreams)
(2010)

Undiscovered dreams
An unexpected journey
Drifting along memories and hopes
A sweet yearning

Of what could be

Should be

May still

All there for my eye to see
In this painting on the wall.

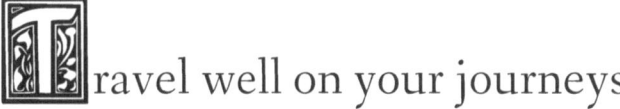

Travel well on your journeys

What you find cannot be guessed

What you leave cannot be known truly

Yet somehow between the unforeseen and the unknown

We meet.

In that meeting, swift or long

We make a difference in one another's song

In that brief breath when the past says goodbye

When the future is a flicker ahead

We pause time

Thank you for lingering this moment in mine.

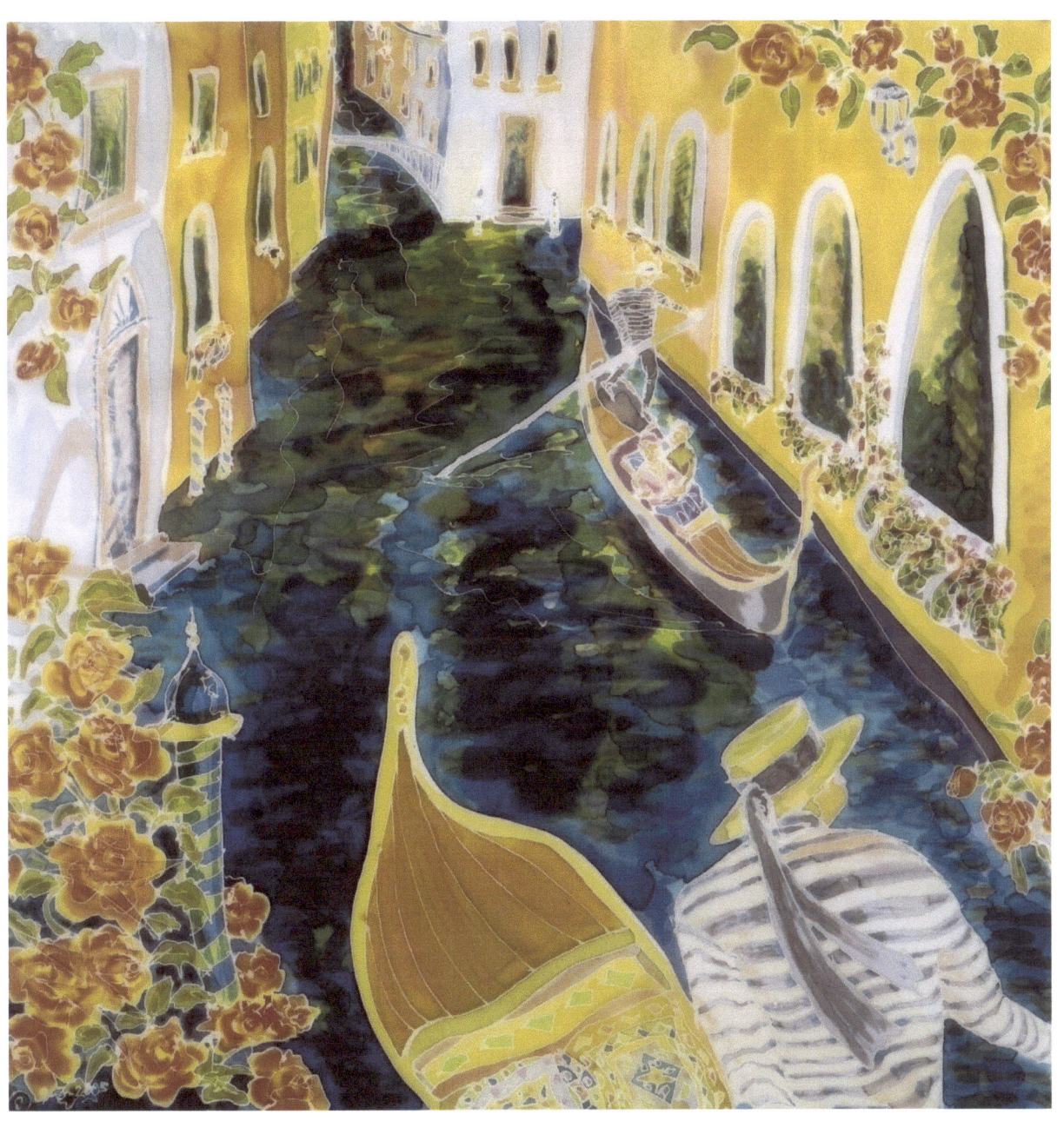

GONDOLIER OF VENICE
(2005)

About the Artist

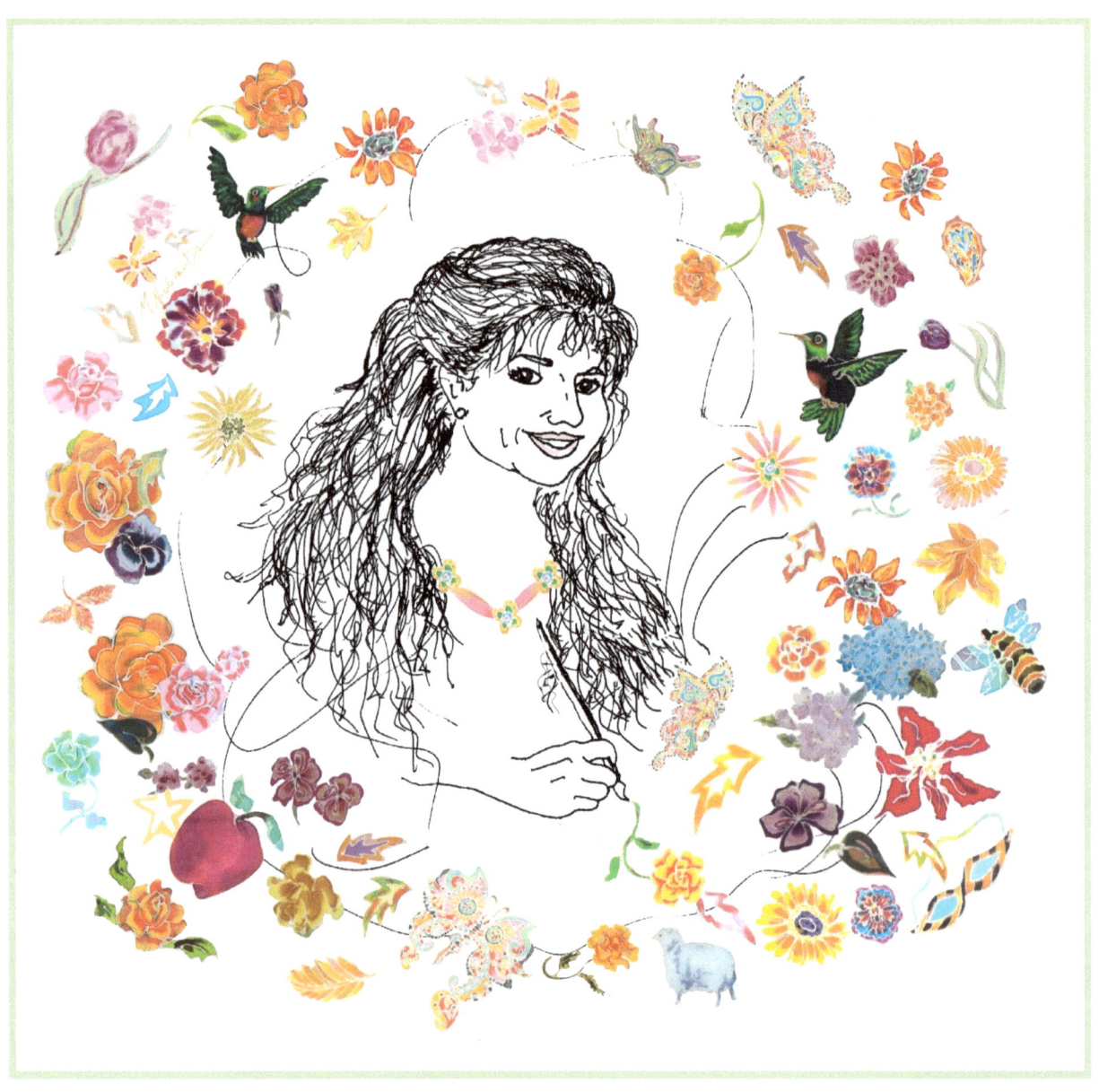

SELF PORTRAIT
(2015)

The artwork, poetry and writings you find in this book are by the artist and author M. Nicole van Dam. Nicole is inspired by the lively beauty of the world around us and by the artistry of the great Impressionists. Nicole works in many media, such as oils, acrylics, water color, pastels, and pen and ink. Nicole is a California native born of Dutch immigrant parents. She was educated on the East Coast and is now living by California's Central Coast with her much-loved husband, dogs and bird.

Nicole celebrates life's beauty, engaging us with joyful colorful expression in both words and art. In addition to this book, Nicole has also written other books, including both children's book and adult books, all lovingly illustrated by Nicole. You can learn more about her children's books at OnceUponaTme.bz and about her adult books at Butterflies.bz. In addition to her writing, Nicole's artwork has been internationally licensed.

To learn more about this engaging artist and author, please visit Nicole.bz. You can also read about Nicole's artistic endeavors, pets and vegetable garden at her various blogs, including our1earth.com and inspirations.bz. If you are interested in seeing Nicole's art portfolio please visit NicolevanDam.com. To purchase Nicole's art and books, please visit create.bz .

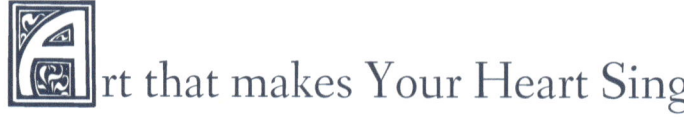Art that makes Your Heart Sing

with the Memory of what could be...

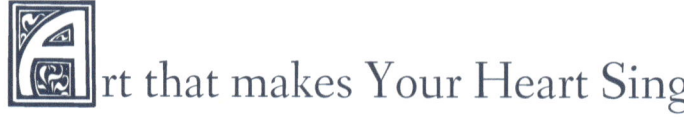

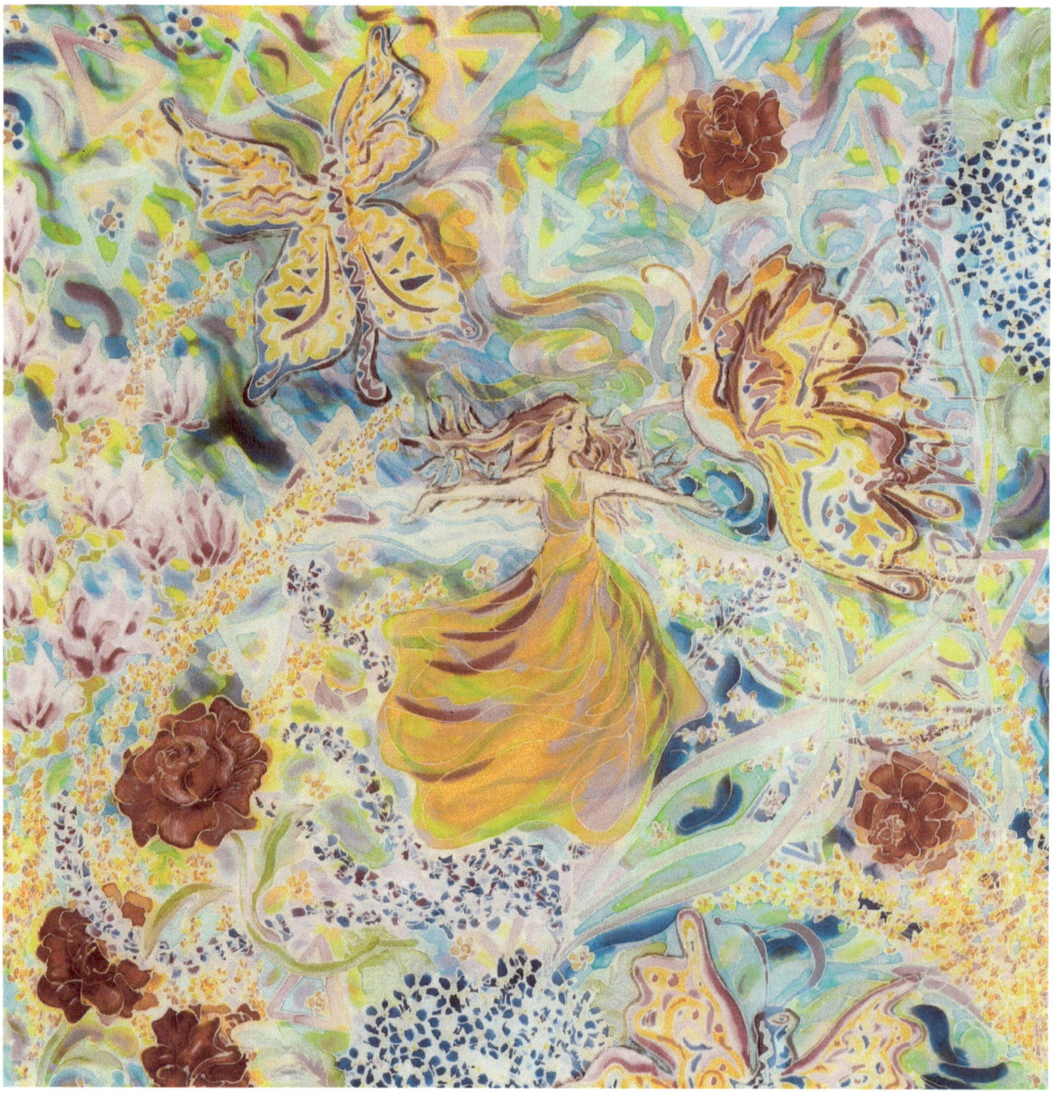

BUTTERFLY WOMAN
(2006)

Thank You for supporting the artwork and creativity of M. Nicole van Dam. We hope that you enjoy this book, and look forward to hearing your thoughts.

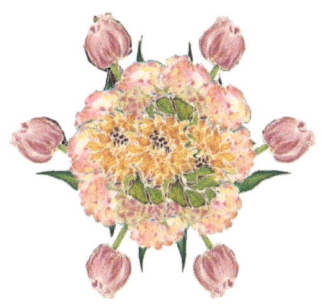

TO CONTACT NICOLE:

M. Nicole van Dam
P.O. Box 583
Ojai, CA 93024

Email: Nicole@Artimagination.com
Website: Artimagination.com
Blog: Wishes.bz

To learn more about this special artist, designer, writer and poet, please visit Artimagination.com or the artist's blog at Wishes.bz.

Cover Art:

JAAAAZZZZ BY M. NICOLE VAN DAM *(2008)*

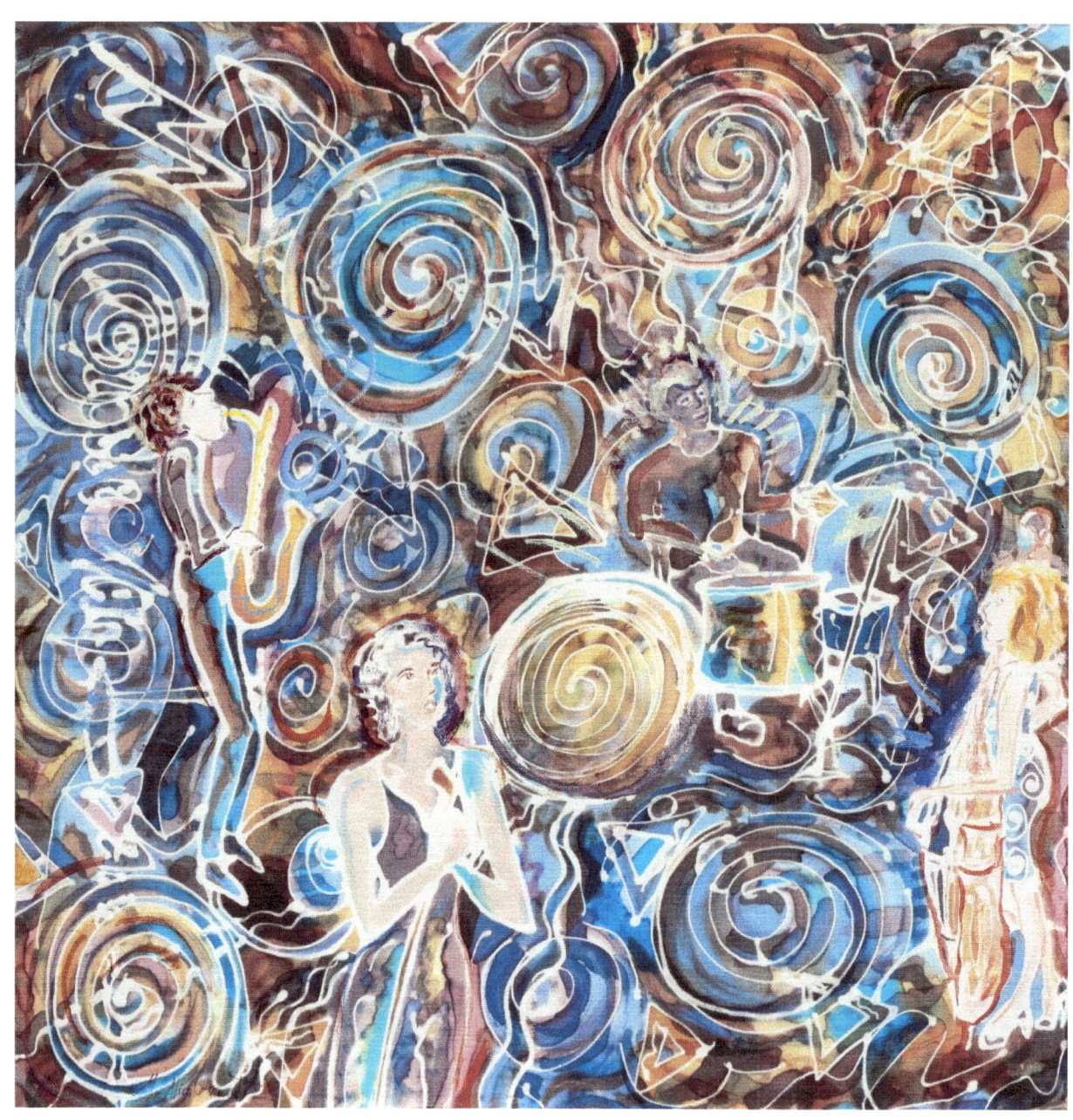

JAAAAZZZZ
(2008)

Dedication

This Book is Dedicated to my Mother and Father

Jetty and Simon van Dam,

who through their support and belief in me

gave me a safe bridge to a new life,

and to my husband

Jay,

who is my new life.

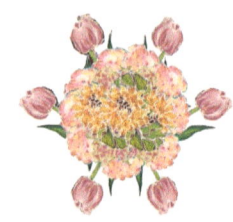

A FEW OF THE OTHER BOOKS FEATURING THE WORKS OF M. NICOLE VAN DAM:

HIGH SPIRITS!

ACHIEVE YOUR GOALS!

INCA DINK, THE GREAT HOUNDINI

THIS LITTLE PUPPY

ROSIE AND EMMA PLANT A SEED

TO LEARN MORE, PLEASE VISIT BUTTERFLIES.BZ